GLORIA'S ROAD: A SCHIZOPHRENIC WOMAN'S PERILOUS PATH TO CHRIST

A memoir

By Gloria Lovejoy

Conquest Publishers
Bladensburg, Maryland

Conquest Publishers
A division of Conquest Industries LLC
P.O. Box 611
Bladensburg, MD 20710-0611
www.conquestpublishers.com

ISBN 10: 0-9656625-8-6
ISBN 13: 978-0-9656625-8-1

Library of Congress Control Number: 2011942957

Printed in the United States of America

Selected Scripture taken from the HOLY BIBLE, NEW INTERNA-TIONAL VERSION®. Copyright © 1973, 1978, 1984 Biblica. Used by permission of Zondervan. All rights reserved.

The ""NIV" and "New International Version" trademarks are regis-tered in the United States Patent and Trademark Office by Biblica. Use of either trademark requires the permission of Biblica.

This book is based on information from the author's own recollections and other sources that the author and publisher believe to be reliable. The author and publisher are not engaged in rendering mental health services, and nothing in this book should be construed to provide or change mental health diagnoses or plans of treatment. If medical, men-tal, professional, or other expert assistance is required by the reader, please seek the services of a competent expert.

Although this book chronicles true events and actual persons, the names of the persons have been changed to preserve their privacy.

*To my mother Esther, who never gave up on my writing,
and the late Reverend Mr. Albert Testa.*

TABLE OF CONTENTS

CHAPTER ONE

A "NORMAL" CHILDHOOD

Click click click click click.

My perception of the sound of Pastor Yeager's shoes on the pavement was far from realistic. To me, it sounded like the Crucifixion, the pounding of nails through the hands of the Lord.

This was the beginning of a nightmare. Everyone in the mental health inpatient unit seemed to be able to read my thoughts.

I described everything as being "muddled." My symptoms were also manifested in visual misperceptions. One of the other patients, for example, showed me a picture of her cat, which appeared to have fluorescent green eyes that popped out at me . . .

* * *

I was born in a small town in Pennsylvania on September 13, 1959, the first daughter in a family that would eventually grow to have three children. I have an older brother I'll call Johnny; a sister I'll call Peggy came along four years later. Because my brother and I were closer in age than my sister and I, he and I were closer, period. I remember how awesomely protective Johnny was of me.

I felt an incessant need for attention, which often backfired on me. When I was about three, during my potty-training days, I used to lie down and kick and scream until my mom came and pulled my pants up. Finally, one day, she grabbed hold of me and spanked me. Needless to say, I never did it again.

Johnny and I were awakened one night about a year later. "Mom's gonna have a baby!" he exclaimed. One would have thought that I had not even known she was pregnant, because I was genuinely surprised. Looking back, perhaps I had wanted to block it out of my mind because I wanted to be the baby forever.

The idea of a new sister was stressful. The first thing I said after they brought her home from the hospital was *"Eww! She's ugly! Take her back!"* I did not understand the whole concept of pregnancy—I thought my parents just went to the hospital, picked out a baby, and then brought it home. After all, it happened that way in all the cartoons.

I was no longer the baby, and I hated every minute of it. I was extremely jealous of my sister; it was obvious from the way I behaved. It seemed like all the attention that was once given to me was now given to her.

Yet, the first few years with a baby in the house were genuinely neat. Not until later did I begin to torment the poor child. In many families, the older ones pick on the younger ones. Only I went overboard.

I had some pet names for Peggy (short for "Margaret") such as "Migdy," "Pigret," "Digby," and the worst one of all, "Hogtrash." I coined this name when I was cleaning her room, called her "a little hog," and said, "Just look at this trash under your bed!"

One would have thought that I *hated* my sister. I used to take the index finger of my right hand and twirl it around in a little circle. She'd scream. Other times, I was just plain mean to her. Mom used to say that I had given Peggy a complex. Most of the time, I just called her names.

I realized just how much I did love my sister one summer day in 1976, when my parents, my brother, my sister, and I were up at our cabin in the Allegheny Mountains. Peggy came down with intestinal flu and required hospitalization. Dehydrated, and with intravenous needles in her hand, she lay there in bed so pallid. I felt as though her suffering were my fault. I felt guilty for the way I had treated her practically all of her young life. But soon after she recovered, I started tormenting her again.

Mom used to say, "Some people have a mentor—Peggy has a *tormentor.*"

I resented my sister intensely, although she had never really done anything to warrant my resentment. My treatment of her to this day cannot be excused, but beneath it all, I do love her. I feel that her hard-as-nails attitude and genuine lack of compassion for me rests with me alone. A person subjected to the same pain over and over again can eventually become hardened to pain. In fact, she probably has many resentments of her own.

I did something horrible to Peggy once when she was a teenager. She had just come back from the beauty parlor with a new permanent, and she looked very cute. I was standing in the kitchen ironing some clothes. I picked a fight with her and finally threw the hot iron at her, but Mom intervened. That changed Peggy's attitude toward me immensely. She never forgave me; she says that some things cannot be forgiven.

The intense animosity between us will probably never be resolved. My sister has harbored a grudge that she will probably go to her grave bearing. As far as she is concerned, she's stuck with me as a sister and doesn't want me as a friend.

CHAPTER TWO

MY PARENTS

In the spring of 1967, my father, a sheet metal layout worker, was stricken with a ruptured appendix.

He developed peritonitis, ileitis, and phlebitis as well. [1] My brother and I were staying at our grandparents' house, and Poppy called us into a room together and said, "Your daddy might die."

At the age of seven, I was too young to understand death. Death was something that happened to somebody when he or she got really old. My daddy was only in his early twenties.

Dad was in the hospital for twenty-one days. Although he did not die physically, in my mind, I thought he had died. All I knew was that Daddy was away for what seemed like a very long time. I was frightened.

When he got home from the hospital, he was very thin. It truly was a miracle that our daddy was alive. The doctor had even said that it was in the Lord's hands.

Two years after my father's surgery, my mother got very depressed. She had a weight problem. My parents' marriage was on the rocks. Mom had an obsession with an old boyfriend, the birth of my sister, and an incident that occurred when she was a child. All these things contributed to her depression.

---

1   Peritonitis: inflammation of the membrane that lines the cavity of the abdomen; ileitis – inflammation of a section of the small intestine; and phlebitis – inflammation of the veins.

Mom and Dad fought constantly during this time—they even discussed divorce.

It seemed as though I was always in the middle, trying to get them to patch things up and to start loving each other again.

Mom eventually lost her weight through strict dieting and exercise. But after she reached her goal, Dad was jealous of her. He actually seemed to *want* her to be fat. I think that Dad was afraid that Mom would look good to other men. He was insecure. He was more comfortable with a wife who was on the heavy side. That way, no man would be a threat to him.

In 1972, right after Hurricane Agnes, my father had a mental breakdown. I couldn't figure out why there had to be so much family bickering when a family member had an emotional crisis, but it happened again.

My parents separated this time. Dad went to live with my grandparents. It was very hurtful for all three of us. I can't speak for Johnny and Peggy; only for myself. I felt that if Daddy could quit loving Mom, he could also quit loving *me*.

Dad was down at Grammy's for about a month. He came back home after Mom took Johnny, Peggy, and me to Trenton, New Jersey, to see one of Mom's cousins over Labor Day weekend that year.

The fighting never seemed to come to an end. I remember saying, "Here we go again!" each time my parents started fighting.

I was stressed out—even at the age of twelve. I was confused by my parents' marital problems. Why did they have to fight so much?

I grew up thinking that no one liked me. I wasn't interested in football games, roller skating, or anything the other kids did. Instead, I studied all the time. I didn't particularly like the idea of associating with some of the people who hung out in those places anyway.

CHAPTER THREE

MELISSA SMITH

Friends were something I craved—I wanted to be popular. Melissa Smith was my way to popularity. After all, her father was the mayor.

Melissa's mother was an ex-mental patient, and her father was abusive.

As far back as the sixth grade, Melissa was the ringleader of all the girls in my class. Anybody who crossed her went to the torture chamber. Most of the girls in our class got on the bandwagon—doing whatever she said. I was the object of ridicule more than once. I was so sensitive that I didn't even *want* to go to school.

Melissa used to wait in the bathroom at school. When I came in, she would dip toilet paper in the commode and throw it at me—all in the name of *fun!*

I put myself on the line for this little witch. I was afraid of her. I felt that I *had* to be her friend. If I wasn't, she might have done something heinous to me. Or at least that is what I thought. She thought she could mold me into someone who would suit her own purposes. In junior high, I helped Melissa and others cheat on history and math tests—I felt like I had to. I also fell prey to her sick desire to enslave me. I did not feel like a friend. I felt more like a victim. From the ages of twelve to fifteen, I began to have severe bouts of depression, most of which I thought were the result of Melissa's bullying.

But Melissa's own life also contained sadness. She told me that she used to pull her hair out, and that her father once took her to the barbershop to get her head shaved. He also kept her locked in her bedroom most of the time.

I didn't particularly *like* Melissa Smith. She threatened to get me arrested for slander for comments like telling her that her sister was on drugs. And I was intimidated by her threats. When she called me on the phone, I told whoever answered to tell her I wasn't home. Then I took the call anyway. I imagined that she *knew* I was lying. It was utter paranoia.

In tenth grade, I became so depressed that I wanted to commit suicide. I considered killing Melissa Smith, but realized that I would be better off if I killed myself. I didn't want to be incarcerated in a juvenile detention center.

Finally, I told my mother I needed a psychiatrist. She made an appointment for me to see the head of the outpatient department at a nearby hospital. Two weeks later, I was admitted to the psychiatric ward there.

CHAPTER FOUR

HOSPITALIZED

I walked down the corridor of the psychiatric unit at Mercy Hospital. One of the first people I met was Craig Bower, a short young man with long, blondish-brown hair. He was a psychiatric aide in the unit, and he encouraged me to write poetry as a way to express my feelings. I saw people much worse off than myself, and I began to count my blessings.

After a few weeks of writing poetry with Craig, I believed that I had fallen in love with him. I was *obsessed* with him. Perhaps it was nothing more than a fixation. Nevertheless, I thought Craig Bower was the greatest.

Not long after I met Craig, I met Ruth Jones, a woman with long, black hair who had been found sleeping in a nearby hotel bathroom. She was screaming wildly. Perhaps her first impression of the psychiatric ward was different from mine, because her first stop was isolation, where she was locked up. Her physical problems seemed to affect her mentally, and some people— both staff and patients—treated her badly.

Looking at me one day, she said, "And you. You're a premed student in psychology who is traveling incognito, investigating the patients."

Ruth Jones was probably the sickest person in the unit at that time. One evening she was misbehaving, and again it was necessary for them to drag her off to isolation. She asked me to help her. I refused.

Ruth died shortly thereafter.

Next I met Matt Weston, a sixteen-year-old boy who I thought looked like Robby Benson. He was a very intelligent young man. We were friends for a long time after we were discharged, but we fell apart when he was arrested for possession of a controlled substance in the early 1980s.

Carly Beckman was twenty-five, and my roommate for most of my thirty-three- day stay at Mercy Hospital. At first, she seemed okay, but the longer I knew her, the more my patience wore thin. But we were friends for a while after we were discharged.

I remember watching Darla Peterson sit on the floor in the hallway and burn dozens of holes in her hands, seeming to feel no pain. One day, she slashed her wrist with the tab of a soft-drink can.

Darla and I competed for Craig Bower's attention. I even wrote a poem about the anger I felt toward her:

Ire
Full of anger
Overheated
That it cannot
Be depleted.
This is my head
As it is now
To cool it down,
I know not how.

Darla Peterson was a mixed-up kid. She was out of control. I feel that she made her problem much worse for herself than it actually was. Most of us did.

The second-to-last person on my list of mentally disturbed cronies was Paula Rossi, a black woman who had multiple sclerosis. She was married to an Italian American.

Paula was a real sweetie. I recall helping her get from one room to the next. In a manner of speaking, she was pathetic.

I remember how she used to threaten to "jam my jaws" whenever I talked about suicide.

I loved Paula. Being from a town the size of Port Trevorton, where there were no black people, and the typical inhabitant was bigoted, I knew that having a friend like Paula was a way for me to break down the prejudicial barriers that had been formed in my mind by my upbringing. I no longer *stared* at black people. It was a good experience. I came to realize that regardless of race, creed, or color, everyone is a human being, and everyone is deserving of respect.

Finally, there was Willard Franklin, who was in a world all his own. I was unable to communicate with Willard—I assume he was schizophrenic. He was eventually transferred to Harrisburg State Hospital.

* * *

Most of the people I met during my first hospitalization were much sicker than I was. Some of them helped me without even knowing it.

After a month of group therapy, one-on-one counseling, medicinal therapy, and writing poetry, I began to prepare for discharge. I really did not want to go back to school again. My fear of Melissa Smith had not been resolved. I really believed that she would do something abominable to me.

After I started back to school again and dropped all the minor subjects so I could catch up on the major ones—and also having been switched over to the other academic section—I realized with the help of my therapist that my fears were all irrational. The separation from Melissa Smith was all that I needed.

My parents, my brother, my sister, and I went to family therapy once a week for about six months after I was discharged. I could not see how my family had anything to do with my immediate problem, but Mrs. Swisher, our therapist, felt that we all had a hand in it. She also wanted to show my family how they could help me.

I started a project for the school nurse, Anita Phillips. It was a watercolor of a fruit basket. Someone stole it before I could get it finished. Working on it, though, I learned that the key to recovery was keeping busy.

CHAPTER FIVE

EXPERIMENTING WITH DRUGS

While walking up the street one day, I saw a young man I knew from the hospital, Dave Koch, who'd had an appendectomy while I was being treated for rheumatic fever.

I hopped in his car with Dave and three other men, and this was the first time I smoked pot. I went home that night knowing that the house we lived in was not big enough for me to avoid my mother meeting me at the door. The first things she asked were: "Have you been drinking?" and "Why are your eyes so glassy?"

I didn't deny any of it. I told her I was drunk and had been smoking pot.

She marched me into the therapist's office a few days later and said, "Tell her what you've been up to."

"I got drunk the other night and tried pot," I said.

"Why did you do that?" asked Mrs. Swisher, the therapist.

"I wasn't in my right frame of mind," I said.

"That won't work with me," she scolded. But I didn't learn my lesson until years later.

At first I was just a social partier, but soon I was addicted to alcohol and amphetamines, and I developed a psychological dependence on marijuana. I used pot to escape the pain of reality, and it's my belief that I used drugs and alcohol for medicine. I had no sooner recovered from the breakdown when I started running around with drug addicts and alcoholics—and using with them.

I had my first sexual experience when I was sixteen. Rick Brown was his name, and he was twenty-seven. In fact, most of my boy-friends were six to fourteen years older than I.

I thought I loved him, but he was definitely a loser. I thought the way he was with women was the way *all* men were with women. I also thought that women were supposed to juggle men like tennis balls. I was very impressionable, so I did it, too. Rick was a terrible influence on me—a one-night stand *twice,* so to speak. Neither of us actually broke it off.

I was used, dumped, and given no explanation.

Sexually and romantically, I was definitely off to a bad start. What's more, I could not have sex without feeling guilty because of the good moral standards my parents had instilled in me. Having a great need for acceptance and wanting to be liked, I felt I had no other choice but to sleep with almost every guy I went out with. I actually lost count of the number of men.

I did not know how to handle a date with a *nice* guy. For some reason, I could not even kiss a *nice* guy without reducing him—in my mind—to someone who deserved no respect whatsoever.

During the middle of my senior year in high school, I started having an affair with Rick's brother Larry. I was as close to being in love with Larry as I had been with Rick.

CHAPTER SIX

NO LONGER A WOMAN!

I was a seventeen-year-old girl having an affair with a thirty-six-year-old man. The sad part of it was that he was married and had two children, one from a former marriage and one with his current wife.

The physical part of the relationship ended on September 2, 1978, two days before I enlisted in the U.S. Army. I thought I was pregnant and that the army would give me an abortion. I was also running away from Larry.

The two nights before my departure from Pennsylvania to Fort McClellan in Alabama were spent with Alan Peterson. He took me barhopping and smoked pot with me. He gave me an ounce for a going-away present, which I, in turn, divided among my friends. I certainly could not take it with me.

September 27 came and went. Sergeant Fisher, my recruiter, and I had an agreement about certain things I had written on my enlistment contract that defrauded the U.S. Army. The agreement was that I would be silent, while he would conceal the truth.

I was no longer a woman. I was a soldier.

Among other things that officers talked about during processing at the reception station were penalties for fraudulent enlistment. I got scared. They mentioned a $20,000 fine and five years in prison. The next day was more of the same.

I was terrified.

The third day at the reception station, I turned myself in to the liaison officer for twenty-two counts of fraud. I lied about every illness I had ever had and my drug and alcohol problems. I believe that on the questionnaire I filled out for the security clearance I needed for my MOS, or military occupational specialty, there was the question: "Have you ever told a lie?" I said, "No."

Who in the world was going to believe *that?*

I was pulled from training on the fifth day and termed a holdover. On the sixth day, I was put back into training, where I remained for the next ten days. The Department of the Army was waiting for my medical records to be forwarded to them, and in the meantime, I was at the mercy of my overbearing drill instructor, Sergeant Todd, who was notorious for being the toughest drill sergeant in our company. I was convinced that he hated me and that he singled me out to give me another breakdown.

I could not march. I did not know my left foot from my right, nor could I do *one* push-up. We were in physical training one day, and I was out of sync with the rest of the company. Drill Sergeant Todd downed me for push-ups. I lay there on my belly like a snake, with my right leg shaking like crazy.

Drill Sergeant Todd screamed, *"Private Lovejoy, you ain't even fit to be in the*
  f—ing army!"

After ten days as a trainee, I was demoted to holdover again, and there I remained until my discharge on December 6. Basically, I did detail, KP duty, and answered the phones in the orderly room. As my company commander told me, I was earning my room and board.

Soon after I was put in holdover, I was given liberty passes every weekend.

I spent them getting drunk. My promiscuity took its toll. My life could be described as a big mess.

I called my mother late one night and told her that I was an alcoholic. That particular night, I drank half of a fifth of rum. I was so drunk I couldn't stand up for very long, and the headache I had the next morning made me feel as if my head was in a vise. I had never been so intoxicated in my life. I knew I had a drinking problem, but I did nothing about it until years later.

I hated myself so much that I could not stand to look in the mirror anymore.

My weekends were spent drinking, smoking pot, and having sex with practically any man who would have me. My self-esteem was at an all-time low. I had no respect for myself at all. I was so caught up in this insane lifestyle that I did not care whether I messed up or not. What's more, I didn't even realize that I was bent on self-destruction.

I didn't think there was a nice person left on the face of the earth. I thought everybody drank the way I did, used drugs the way I did, and slept around the way I did.

We are judged by the company we keep. It is difficult to love others when we do not love ourselves.

CHAPTER SEVEN

FRED RUSH

One night in November 1978, while I was still in the army, I met Fred Rush. He stood across from me in the pool hall at the 1-2-3 Club. He was not the most handsome man in the world, yet he was good-looking in a rugged way. He was a little over six feet tall and had brown eyes, brown hair, and a moustache.

I started talking to him, and he offered to buy me a beer. After which, we went into the disco and danced. Within days, I fell prey to his animal magnetism. We were in his room at the 356th Transportation Co. soon after, making love. Although we had been acquainted for only a very short period of time, we were very fond of each other.

One night, he caught me sitting on another guy's lap. In fact, he caught me sitting with two different guys on two different occasions. Had I known that Fred was a one-woman man at the beginning, I would never have put myself in a position to almost lose him.

Eventually, I was forced to choose between Fred and one of the guys he caught me sitting with, Will Thompson. Needless to say, I chose Fred after calling a conference with a friend I had met in Sergeant Todd's platoon. Her name was Danielle Jackson. Danielle was a crazy young black woman who had been my best friend while I was at Fort McClellan. She was crazy in what some might call an aggressive way. For example, she pointed an M-16 rifle right between my eyes. I didn't know if it had live ammo or not. All I knew was that we were assigned to armed-guard duty, and she had locked and loaded.

Danielle told me that Fred cared about me more than he cared to admit, and that Will just wanted to use me.

Fred and I saw each other about three nights a week until December 6, when I was discharged. On the plane back north, I decided that it was just an army romance, and that was where it ended. But soon after I got home, I wrote to Fred to tell him that I loved him, and that I wanted him to be a part of my life. A little buzzer had gone off in my head while I was at work one day, and for a very long time afterward, he was all I could think about.

I received one letter from Fred. It was a heartbreaker, since it was the last.

It took months for me to get over Fred—yet I never *really* got over him. I wished I had done things differently, as far as he was concerned. My promiscuity took its toll on my relationships with more than one man. Most of the men in my life hated this character defect of mine. Why couldn't I stop? I just wanted to be loved and accepted by a man, but it seemed as though I could not be the kind of woman men wanted. I was good for only one thing—a roll in the hay.

Many of the men I got involved with pressured me to have sex with them, and after I did it, they said I was too easy. Fred was not like that. He forgave me over and over again. He certainly tolerated more from me than I would have tolerated from him.

CHAPTER EIGHT

BARRY SNYDER

I met Barry Snyder at the Snyder family reunion the summer before. They showed me a picture of him. I had seen him at the store where I worked, so the next time he came in, I introduced myself. Barry Snyder turned my life around. *He took the brightest smile in town. He took it, and he turned it upside down*, to paraphrase a Gregg Allman song.

Barry and I had a good relationship for a while. After I found out that I could not reduce him to an object of contempt, I could no longer treat him amicably. In fact, no one in the world would tolerate as much mental cruelty as I subjected Barry to. What I did to Fred Rush was nothing compared to the abuse Barry withstood.

We were together for a grand total of six months. I thought that I loved him, but I couldn't respect him because his mother was in control of his mind and his life. It used to disgust me—the way she kissed him on his neck and treated him like a 175-pound baby. She was in the driver's seat. She called the shots. To put it bluntly, Barry was a mama's boy.

His mother's interference in our relationship, along with my sick desire to hurt Barry, served only to break his morale. He was miserable in our relationship. He ended it once a few months before Christmas, and ended it finally at Christmastime. I asked for another chance, which proved fruitless.

I was insane that bleak Christmas night in 1979. I threatened to shoot Barry. I slapped him across the face, and I called him a homosexual because we had never really had a sexual relationship.

I then called the Crisis Intervention Center, where the uncle of my best friend volunteered, and tried to get myself committed. I took off like a shot out the door, got in my car, and sped down the road at 65 miles per hour. The speed limit was 45. Barry followed me to a nearby exit. He had to get gas, so he couldn't follow me all the way to the crisis center.

Love and hate cannot be mixed, yet somehow they can coexist. One cannot love without a certain amount of vulnerability.

Had I the opportunity to do it over again, I would have handled things quite differently.

I felt mental anguish as a result of the pain I had inflicted on Barry. I was mean to him, pure and simple. My pain was well deserved. In fact, part of me may never forgive myself.

CHAPTER NINE

THE RUINATION

Soon after Barry Snyder and I broke up, I started dating Ken Kirshner, one of the biggest burnouts in town. One of the most prominent things I remember about Ken is that he came to pick me up for a date one night, and he had no hair. The idiot had shaved his head.

Ken was a good candidate for a mental hospital. He was, in every sense of the word, crazy. Basically, our relationship consisted of getting drunk, getting high, and having sex. Ken was insane. On New Year's Eve one year, he dressed up as the New Year's baby, complete with a diaper. He stopped at the store where I worked to show me his costume. My reaction? He's *wacko!*

Ken was incapable of holding down a job. He quit one job while I was seeing him. He was living at home at the time, and he didn't want his parents to know, so he used to go to Hendershodt's Bar & Grill every day during the hours that he would normally have been at work. He blew out the engine of his car for failing to keep oil in it, and it sat out in his parents' yard for what seemed like years. His ex-wife described him as being "worse than worthless."

So, why did I love him so much? *He made me feel like I was beautiful.* Despite his genuine lack of insight, he sensed that I had a poor self-image. He told me I was okay, and he made me feel wanted and accepted.

One week while I was seeing Ken, in addition to sleeping with him, I slept with at least six other men, and I contracted gonorrhea. I practically overdosed on penicillin to get rid of it. I knew I had it, but assumed it was pelvic inflammatory disease, which I had suffered from once before. (I wasn't aware that gonorrhea may cause PID.) After taking penicillin for about two weeks, I went to get tested. I must have just hit the right dosage, because my test came back negative. Ken's best friend, Alan Peterson, caught it, but since my test came back negative, I let Al think that he had caught it from Donna, his other girlfriend.

He kept saying, "She's not like that!"

I kept asking, "Are you sure?"

I was a slut in every sense of the word. I had this great need to be loved and accepted, but when it was handed to me, I was terrified of it. I really *did* desire emotional attachments.

Surprisingly enough, Ken was fortunate *not* to have caught VD from me. "God gave me a brain," he said, before he got tested, "but I never learned how to use it." He then asked me to shoot him.

This was a nightmare. It was the pits. I had hit bottom. It was obvious that I was destroying myself.

* * *

Night after night, my mother lay awake worrying about me while I was out carousing. Night after night, she prayed to God that I would make it home without dying in an accident. Her greatest hope was that I would find God. And that with His help, I would find victory over my drug and alcohol problems and my promiscuity. It seemed as though she did not know what to do. She felt like she was sitting idly by, watching her daughter go down the tubes.

She threatened to kick me out of the house. She threatened to charge me room and board. She tried everything. What was lacking? She loved me. Was love enough?

Speaking from a daughter's point of view, I always felt like I had to sneak out on dates. I didn't even like to bring my boyfriends home because Mom felt a great need to show the family albums and the ones with pictures of our trip to Wyoming and Yellowstone National Park in 1978—the trip of a lifetime for Mom and Dad.

My mom always made me feel like sex is dirty. I guess I was trying to prove her wrong. Not only did she make me feel it was dirty, but she and her sisters made me ashamed of my breasts. They got me down on the floor and looked at them when I first started to develop. As a result, I do not stand up straight to this very day. At first, it made me want to hide my breasts. Over the years, slouching became a habit. That was not the only reason for my slouching, though. I was also the tallest girl at school.

Each time I had sex, I felt like my mother was there—watching me. As a result, I got no enjoyment out of it. Not only that, I was not very selective. Some of the men I had sex with were downright slovenly, while others were so-called "upstanding citizens of the community." I slept with men from all walks of life, including a minister's son. The only difference between a prostitute and me was that I did not charge anything.

My drug problem got worse and worse. I could not stand to look in the mirror anymore. I hated myself. I couldn't have cared less whether I lived or died. I was also "crazy."

During the summer of 1980, I suddenly became concerned with morality. Believe it or not, I actually *wanted* to be a good person.

I was having an affair with Bob Hatton, one of the town's police officers—maybe because I wanted to protect myself from being arrested. Every time we got together, I told him that I wanted to be a good girl. Bob had a wife and two children. I knew this relationship would also lead nowhere, which is why it was important for me to work on a self-improvement course. At one time, it would not have fazed me to be involved with a married man. Now it seemed important for me to clean up my act.

Whenever I told Bob that I wanted to be a good girl, he'd say, "You're good," and then he continued to seduce me.

After sex, I felt terrible—as dirty and as cheap as I did with most of the men I had slept with. For me, sex was never a consummation of love. It was "animal sex." The men I got involved with had no desire for emotional attachment. I wanted to be emotionally involved with some of them, but I didn't know how to ask for intimacy. It's my belief that we all need and want to be loved, except for, perhaps, a sociopath or psychopath.

I was a very messed-up young lady, but the desire to be "good" became increasingly important. Looking back, I can see God's hand at work.

CHAPTER TEN

THE CONVICTION OF THE HOLY SPIRIT

In the autumn of 1980, I was up to my usual tricks in my hometown. I'll mention the cannabis plants that sprouted in a planter in the police station there, compliments of Yours Truly. It was my idea, and Al Peterson, who lived just two blocks from the station, came along and, well, *went* along. It was late one night when we stuck just a few little seeds under the soil of the planter. We were probably wasted.

I can't recall how long it took for our sowing to bear fruit, so to speak, but what I do know is that one day the chief of police came to the movie theater where I worked and suggested that I had had something to do with that illicit little greenhouse experiment.

I had heard of corruption in the police department, and I wondered if they took some out and smoked it.

In October 1980, I went to a party one night down by the river with Al Peterson. As usual, I got totally inebriated. When the party was half over, Ken Kirshner and Don Firsching asked me to give them a ride to Rocky's, a bar on the outskirts of town.

I was so drunk and high that I almost drove my car through the back of the bar.

Ken told Don to take over, but I said I'd be okay. I had an ounce of pot on me, so Don and I went out to get high. We went to a little road out in the country where all the partiers and parkers went. I got my car stuck and had to ask Don to get it out.

The very next day, while I was standing in the bathroom combing my hair, a feeling of love came over me that cannot be described in words. I knew that it was God, and I knew that it was love. *"God is love!"* I exclaimed to my image in the mirror.

That was the Holy Spirit, and He was giving me a taste of what God is like.

A second thought came to mind: "What kind of drug did I get hold of last night?" This was the enemy, whispering in my ear. He wanted me to continue in my lifestyle of insanity.

I came to realize that the reasons for my concern for morality and virtue were a direct result of God's hand in my life.

I liked the feeling of love and wanted it for always, so I made an appointment to talk to our pastor. I told him that my life was straightening out gradually, and I told him about the feeling of love. I told him that I wanted that feeling permanently.

He said, "I think you may have had a religious experience. Have you ever considered receiving Jesus Christ as your Savior?"

My first thought was, "Quaker meeting has begun. No more laughing, no more fun." But I reluctantly, halfheartedly, repented.

On the way home, I was under the intense conviction to do it and make it stick. A still, small voice from within said, "Come unto me as a little child."[2] This was the Lord's invitation.

I sat down at the supper table that night, more and more pressed to listen to that invitation. Suddenly I said, "Excuse me, I have to go to my room and take care of something."

In my room, I got down on my knees and said these words: *"God, I am a sinner. Please forgive me for all of my sins. Jesus, be the Lord of my life."*

That was on January 11, 1981.

---

2   See Matthew 19:14, Mark 10:14, and Luke 18:16, NIV.

CHAPTER ELEVEN

A BORN-AGAIN CHRISTIAN

Joy filled my heart. Love ruled my life. I was a born-again Christian now.

I told my mother I wanted to join the church. My first task was to become a member of the choir. The office of Sunday school treasurer followed.

But by mid-February, my joy was turning into sorrow. I became convinced that I had committed the unpardonable sin of blasphemy against the Holy Spirit, and I kept hearing an audible voice that seemed very real. And then it was a temptation, and the temptation was so overwhelming that I muttered some things under my breath.

On March 1, 1981, I said to my mother, "I blasphemed against the Holy Spirit."

Concerned about what I was experiencing, in a very angry voice, Mom said, "Gloria, you need professional help!" All I ever needed to do was express my mental anguish, and doing that was grounds for even *more* mental abuse!

I went to work that morning as usual, but I couldn't work, so I drove myself up to Mercy Hospital. When I got there, I voiced my complaints to the crisis-intervention caseworker, and he arranged for me to be admitted to the psychiatric unit.

I went up to the second-floor unit with Mike Woodard, the caseworker. This was on a Sunday, so I wouldn't get a chance to talk to a psychiatrist until the next day.

The first thing I did after going through admissions was get on the telephone.

I called at least twenty ministers and asked them all the same question. Had I blasphemed the Holy Spirit? They all said the same thing: "If you had blasphemed the Holy Spirit, you wouldn't even be concerned about it."

It didn't matter how many times I heard the same thing. I was bound and determined to believe that there was no hope for me, and that I was headed for hell.

On Monday I called twenty more ministers, some of whom I had called the day before. By the end of the week I had called at least one hundred ministers, all of whom told me that the very fact that I was concerned about it proved that I was not guilty of the unpardonable sin.

In addition to calling every minister in town, I called some collect or billed the call to my parents' phone. When ministers visited other patients, I cornered them and asked the same question.

By the end of the week, the staff restricted my visitors to family. I sneaked phone calls, even though they were also restricted.

At the end of two weeks, after being diagnosed with a schizophrenic disorder, I was discharged—feeling the same as when I was first admitted.

My first weekend home proved disastrous. I scratched my wrist with a razor blade. We went to my brother's house later that night, a Sunday, and I made a long-distance call on his phone to a minister in a town eleven miles away. My brother screamed, "I'm going to knock some sense into you!" Johnny is 6' 4" tall and doesn't know his own strength. He beat me up bad. His beating left a bruise on my neck the size of a grapefruit.

The strange thing was, I didn't even defend myself.

I screamed, "Go ahead and kill me! I deserve to die for what I've done!"

Dr. Peterman, the psychiatrist who was taking care of my medication in the outpatient clinic, said I should press charges, but how can somebody press charges against her brother?

Within days, I was a patient in the psychiatric unit at Mercy

Hospital again. My doctor was Dr. Peterman, a tall, rather heavy-set man who reminded me of Colonel Sanders.

Once again, I called minister upon minister. I asked the same question over and over. Always the same reply: "The very fact that you are concerned about it proves that you have not blasphemed the Holy Spirit."

I had developed an obsession. Not only that, I was terrified. I found myself uttering curse words against the Holy Spirit. I had literally lost control, and I was getting more and more frightened. I had also developed a compulsion to utter ridiculous, nonsensical words against the Holy Spirit. These words were not coming from a wicked heart; they were coming from a compulsion and a thought disorder. I was a very sick young lady who was not even being held accountable by God because of her impaired mental state.

Again, my diagnosis was a schizophrenic disorder. I participated in the various groups, crafts, and other activities as part of my therapy. At the end of two weeks, my parents were not satisfied with my progress. They arranged for me to be transferred to a drug and alcohol rehabilitation center.

While there, I felt like a zombie—a hollow, empty shell just walking around.

I believe I felt this way because I had blasphemed the Holy Spirit. Dr. Dave Beagley, a psychologist, was called in to consult with me for a few minutes. I had heard that Dr. Beagley was a Christian, so my first question, naturally, was: "Did I blaspheme the Holy Spirit?"

"I just want you to forget about that for a minute," he said.

Within minutes, he made arrangements for me to be transferred to Hunsinger Medical Center, and the next day my parents drove me there.

* * *

When I arrived at Hunsinger, my mom and dad asked, "Do you

promise to let them help you? Are you going to try?"

The first thing I did was talk to the treatment team. My psychiatrist's name was Dr. Doebler, a woman. I also had a psychiatrist named Dr. Wintersteen, who was in charge of my medication.

I was prescribed Haldol, and I had a bad reaction to it—a seizure. My jaw tightened, my head went back, and I couldn't keep my elbow from jerking up in the air.

I was basically miserable.

Dr. Wintersteen gave me a shot of Cogentin in a vein of my right arm.

"That ought to fix you up," he said.

Three days later, I requested a transfer to Harrisburg State Hospital. I wanted to go there to "stay 'til the Second Coming of Christ, so I could repent of all my sins.

When my parents heard the news, they were devastated. My mother cried for weeks. She was reliving her father's institutionalization. My grandfather, also a schizophrenic, had been institutionalized for twenty years.

CHAPTER TWELVE

HARRISBURG STATE HOSPITAL

My first stop was the Admissions lobby. Here, I talked to one of the doctors I'd seen at Hunsinger—Dr. Mendez. He talked to me for about fifteen minutes and automatically concluded that I was suffering from a schizophrenic disorder.

A chamber of horrors. That was my first impression of the State Hospital. A pretty, young blonde woman in seclusion vigorously jumped up and down, screaming. A portable curtain hung in front of the huge, shatterproof glass window of the lockup, behind which she was confined. I was taken to the day room, where all of these ugly, greasy-looking women were sitting in chairs, immobile. The first person I talked to was a middle-aged, gray-haired woman named Pat Bogart. I asked her what her diagnosis was. "Manic depression," she replied. "Why are you here?"

"I blasphemed the Holy Spirit."

In walked a loud, boisterous woman who cussed like your average, everyday, run-of-the-mill witch, and bore no resemblance to a lady. Her name was Norma Jean Brown, and I later learned that she was a convicted murderer from an area women's prison. She had a visible beard, and half of her teeth were missing.

Norma Jean fed my delusional system by continually telling me that *she* was Jesus Christ.

One day I refuted her by telling her that Jesus wouldn't murder a fly, let alone another human being.

She threatened to kill me.

I am convinced that she faked her illness so she could use Harrisburg State Hospital as an escape from prison.

Norma Jean was a lesbian who claimed to be a Roman Catholic. I gave her a friendly hug one day in an attempt to save my life. I found out that the only way to pacify her was to play her game.

I am not a lesbian, nor have I ever had a lesbian relationship, but I did hug Norma Jean on one or two occasions. I *never* had a sexual relationship with her.

There was a girl named Dolly Smith who must have had some kind of sexual problem. One day my parents came to see me, and they were invited to the cafeteria at suppertime to drink a cup of coffee. Dolly went up to my father and whispered in his ear, "Do you like to fool around?"

Dad was embarrassed. "No," he said, "I'm a married man—very married."

Dawn Yokin was a woman who did a daily performance across the dayroom floor. She'd walk so far, raise a foot, and then do it again. It was a ritual for her. I assumed she was obsessive-compulsive. Then there was Bea Martin, who kept yelling at the television and turning it off.

Mary Jeffries, another patient, kept cutting herself. I guess you could say I took lessons from her. One day, I scratched myself with a bobby pin. Another time, I found a washer under the drinking fountain. I sharpened it on the tiles on the wall and cut myself with it.

I was in the right place. I fit in perfectly.

I was prescribed a potent tranquilizer and, started feeling better within days. I was still calling ministers, though, and soon staff restricted my telephone privileges. This time, I was given one call per day. They barred my minister friends from the hospital, except for Pastor Rumford, pastor of our church.

On the third day at Harrisburg State Hospital, I felt the presence of the Holy Spirit for the first time in weeks. I lay on my bed and said, "He hath Beelzebub." At that moment, I felt that the Holy Spirit had left me, so I requested to see the chaplain. Minutes later, in walks Chaplain Blackwell, a tall, muscular, middle-aged man who had a Southern accent you could cut with a knife.

"I blasphemed against the Holy Spirit," I said.

Chaplain Blackwell asked me what I did, and I told him.

"You can't manipulate the Holy Spirit with words," he said. "He's not a fickle Spirit."

Throughout our conversation, I sought reassurance half a dozen times or more. Chaplain Blackwell said, "The unpardonable sin is a lifestyle which takes a lifetime to commit, and if you are God's child, it is impossible for you to commit it."

My medication was changed half a dozen times or more during my first month at the hospital. I also tried to commit suicide half a dozen times.

During the week of the Fourth of July, I signed myself out of Harrisburg against medical advice. They instituted a hearing, and I did not have a leg to stand on. I admitted that since my parents were away, I fully intended to go home and "blow my head off."

I was court-committed for ninety days. Days and weeks passed, and I was always on one-to-one suicide precautions. I had become a very difficult patient—a lousy attitude toward certain staff members, for example.

Approximately halfway through my first hospitalization, Dr. Mendez left. I was then assigned to a new psychiatrist, Dr. Garcia. He was an excellent psychiatrist. He seemed very compassionate and showed consistent interest in my recovery.

Dr. Garcia prescribed a dozen or so different tranquilizers, but none did the trick. He finally concluded that something in the tranquilizers made me more depressed.

Dr. Roy Lehman, my psychologist, hypnotized me to try to put a stop to my curse words against the Holy Spirit and the things that had obsessed me, those blasphemous thoughts that Chaplain Blackwell said God couldn't care less about, but which upset me tremendously. Dr. Lehman gave me spiritual counseling without even being a Christian himself. When I asked him if I had blasphemed the Holy Spirit, he would say, "You seem interested."

That was all I needed to hear. God can help his children even when he's using a nonbeliever. God used Balaam's ass to talk to Balaam, didn't He?

In addition to helping me spiritually, Dr. Lehman helped me realize that I was obsessed with the unpardonable sin because of a guilt complex stemming from a relationship with a Greek guy named Nick Theoriculpous, who cooked in a local Greek restaurant. A sexual relationship with Nick proved to be disastrous because of my Christian principles. Soon after we broke up, I started believing Satan's hideous lie.

Ironically, my own sister moved in on Nick the day after I was admitted to Mercy Hospital. As my mother described it, "Peggy was interested in him." Why on earth would my sister want to have her first sexual experience with one of her own sister's castoffs? I guessed that Mom, Peggy, and Nick had their own set of problems, because Mom was on the warpath. To me, my sister was just opportunistic in wanting to be involved with Nick regardless of the fact that I didn't want him. It added fuel to the fire, so to speak.

She claimed that she just wanted to find out what I saw in him. Mom was right—Peggy was hot for Nick.

In the meantime, my brain felt like it was falling apart. I thought that the Holy Spirit lived in my head, and that He couldn't make up His mind whether to leave me or not. Most of the time, it felt like the top of my head was rising. I believed I had caused the Holy Spirit to have a conniption.

My parents came to see me two or three times a week. I believed they came as often as they could because they were afraid that I would never get out of there.

Dr. Garcia finally put me on a drug called Asendin and another called Ativan. Within weeks I was feeling like my old self again, but for the longest time I still believed that I had blasphemed the Holy Spirit.

I was still calling ministers and charging the calls to my parents' number. After receiving $200 and $300 phone bills every month for three months, they finally got their phone disconnected. I then started calling people collect. I wrote letters to Jimmy Swaggart, Billy Graham, and Oral Roberts. They all wrote back, telling me I had not blasphemed the Holy Spirit and explained to me just what that sin really amounts to.

One thing I learned from calling what seemed like thousands of ministers and laymen and laywomen is that everyone interprets the Bible with a different slant, especially when they interpret the unpardonable sin.

Anyway, the obsession dissipated in time after my psychosomatic delusion disappeared. My interpretation of what had happened was that the Asendin and the Ativan caused my brain to "stop throwing fits."

Either that, or God was done with punishing me.

I blamed God for all my suffering for a while. It seemed easier to use Him as a scapegoat than it was to blame my illness or myself. Chaplain Blackwell, Roy Lehman, Ed Vance, my caseworker, and John Showers, the psychologist who conducted the group therapy sessions that I participated in, and all the other workers at Harrisburg State got me to realize that I was *sick,* and not *evil.* Most of all, God played the role of healer, and in June of 1981 I was the recipient of a huge basket of fruit at the annual Fun Fair.

I shared it with everyone on the ward at snack time until the basket was empty.

After I had been better for a while, I was issued a one-hour progressive grounds privilege, which meant that every day I got an extra hour. I was so happy; I was on my way home. Now I could visit with my family outside. I could hold my two nieces on my lap when my brother brought them along.

And I befriended a young black man by the name of Lionel Wilson, and we fell in love. The Holy Spirit convicted me of our physical relationship, but I persisted in disobeying the Lord. I rationalized what I was doing. I tried to make it seem less wrong—I understood the moral question much better, and I didn't feel I was being used. Lionel *cared.*

Lionel wanted to marry me, but I ended the relationship because

of my parents' feelings on the subject. Being from our small, bigoted town, my parents weren't very understanding. Ending the relationship seemed to be the only way to appease them.

Honoring my parents was—and still is—important to me.

In August of that summer, I was transferred to the open ward. I
was given this privilege for working hard toward recovery. I was
responsible for doing my own laundry, and the door was unlocked
during grounds-card hours. By this time I was spending weekends
at home with my parents, and I was making discharge plans.

On September 5, I was discharged. I left the hospital and started
looking for a job almost immediately. I tried to sell vacuum clean-
ers for Electrolux. This job lasted five days. I was not cut out for
sales.

I was hired as a seamstress at a sewing factory—a job that lasted
three weeks. There was a layoff, and I was one of those not called
back.

I then went to work at a sewing factory, Katrina Manufacturing,
owned by Abraham Stein. Again, my work was excellent—but I
was too slow. Production-line jobs proved to be unsatisfactory.
After Abraham gave me the shaft for three days, I told him, "You
don't want brain-surgeon material for this job—you want a *ro-
bot!*"

At that, I got up and left.

Ironically, my grandmother knew the man. She said, "Sis (my
family nickname), don't feel bad. No one can stand to work for
that man. *Nobody* likes him."

Finally, I answered an ad in the paper. An elderly woman named
Eldora Spring was looking for a live-in housekeeper and compan-
ion. It paid $175 per week, more than I was receiving from unem-
ployment. It was an offer I couldn't refuse.

Mrs. Spring was a very difficult person to work for. She complained about everything. Many times she woke me up in the middle of the night to get her a shot of whiskey. If I didn't come right
away, she'd call me "one hell of a nursemaid!" She said I was
beating a hole in the carpet from walking up and down the stairs.

She also complained about what she considered my excessive use of electricity. In fact, when her minister found out I was working for her, he patted me on the head and said, "God bless you, child!" After three months of this impossible situation, I went back to live with my parents.

In November, I slumped into a severe depression because I couldn't find a suitable job. I attempted suicide.

First, I took an overdose. All they did at the emergency room was induce vomiting, and they put me in intensive care for a few days.

Two weeks later, I got into a terrible fight with my father and slashed my wrist to lay a guilt trip on him. He took me to Community Hospital. The doctor who sutured my wrist made arrangements for me to be admitted to Harrisburg State Hospital.

CHAPTER THIRTEEN

INSANITY

From Community Hospital, I was transferred to Mercy Hospital's psychiatric unit. The first thing Dr. Steinberg did was to put me on one-to-ones, which meant having to sit with an employee of the mental health unit twenty-four hours a day to keep me from hurting myself. A day or two later, the one-on-ones were ended, but I was so utterly deranged that I thought I was receiving messages from God and Satan from the television and radio. There was a song out by Daryl Hall and John Oates called "Maneater." I thought it was about *me,* that *I* was the Maneater. It seemed like that was the only song I heard for what seemed like days. I also believed I'd disproved Satan's veracity, which to me was a whole new religion.

I sat down to write a letter to John Wadsworth, someone I had dated. I wrote:

For everything there is a season and a
reason for every purpose under the sun.
 A time to be born and
A time to die,
A time to reap and
A time to sow,
A time to kill and
A time to heal,
A time to tear down and
A time to build,

A time to weep and
A time to laugh,
A time to mourn and
A time to dance,
A time to scatter stones and
A time to gather them,
A time to embrace and
A time to refrain,
A time to search and
A time to give up searching,
A time to keep and
A time to throw away,
A time to tear and
A time to mend,
A time to be silent and
A time to speak,
A time to love and
A time to hate,
A time for war and
A time for peace.

As I was writing down *Ecclesiastes 3:1-8,* the song by the Byrds[3], "Turn! Turn! Turn!" came on the radio. It seemed to be the only song I heard for days.

My confusion was so great that I could not dial a telephone number without getting the numbers all jumbled. My favorite sentence was. "Everything is muddled," according to Ethel Yeager, pastor of our church.

I felt as though I'd had a head-on collision with the devil and redeemed John's faith in human nature. I thought I had turned John Wadsworth into a child of God. Few of my thought processes

---

3   The song "Turn! Turn! Turn! (to Everything There is a Season)", written by Pete Seeger and covered by the Byrds. The song is almost entirely adapted from the Book of Ecclesiastes.

made any sense. I had tried to give John a "head trip" to get what I wanted.

The entire story of my life was being broadcast over television. When I entered a room full of people at the hospital, they seemed to be able to read my thoughts. I looked at a picture of one of the patient's cats, and it appeared to have fluorescent eyes that popped out at me. Beneath all of these symptoms, there I was, fighting to make my way back to reality. Surprisingly enough, I *knew* I was sick, and therefore couldn't be classified as being truly psychotic.

At this point I was nearing the apex of my insanity. I later learned that "God has no grandchildren." The plot thickened with my insanity. Soon I became violent and had to be locked up in isolation for three days. I recall looking at the fenced-in window in the isolation room and saying, "Joseph Smith is looking at me with his goo-goo eyes." I could see the Crucifixion of Jesus Christ on the cement brick wall of the isolation room. Each time they opened my door for any reason, I tried to break out.

I had to go to the bathroom one night. I yelled out the screened-in window for someone, anyone, to let me use the bathroom. They had locked my bathroom door because I kept banging the toilet seat up and down, saying I was "nailing Christ to the cross." Because no one would unlock my bathroom door, I decided to leave my bowel movement right where I was standing. I then decorated my prison cell with feces. I was told at my commitment hearing that I had been eating feces. Needless to say, I was so happy for the aides, nurses, etc., who had to clean up the mess. I felt they deserved every minute of it because they looked the other way when I told them I had to go to the bathroom.

On one occasion during lockup, one of the male aides slammed my head up against the wall, trying to restrain me. I found it necessary to defend myself, so I kicked him in the groin.

After three days, I was moved back into a regular room, but I wasn't feeling any better. Before I was locked up, Dr. Steinberg had put me on a drug called Triavil, which was of no therapeutic value whatsoever. It seemed that everything that had happened that summer had come to the surface—everything I had read, everything I said or did—even the suicide of a friend who was also a schizophrenic—came back to haunt me. I thought Ricky McClain's death resulted in his spirit taking over *my* spirit in the form of a walk-in, and that was why I was crazy. I had read about such spirits that summer in an occult paperback. I also started believing that Norma Jean Brown was indeed Jesus Christ, and I was prepared to "accept her as my Savior."

I saw the cousin of a guy I had grown up with in the hallway one evening, and I asked her to take me home.

I talked to Dr. Steinberg for what seemed like four or five times a day. One time he asked, "Do you trust me?"

"No, because you're a Jew, and the Jews killed Jesus," I replied.

Dr. Steinberg really was trying to help me, but he just didn't know how. Therefore, he instituted a hearing. I was harmful to other people and myself, so I was in for a long-term hospitalization.

Mom and Dad came to the hearing. After the nurses, the psychiatric aides, and Dr. Steinberg presented their case, my father cried like a baby. He was upset because before I went to the hospital, he and I had had that fight that would have reminded somebody of two dogs growling at each other. Dad seemed to think he could cure me by intimidating me. He yelled very hateful things at me and kept telling me to sit down. I asked him to take me to the hospital, and he kept refusing.

"You're not going to run this family any longer! Now straighten up and fly right!" he yelled, and he stuffed a piece of bread into his bellowing mouth. I thought he was more concerned about his appetite than he was about his daughter's mental condition. He seemed to think he could verbally abuse me into a sane state of mind. I hated his guts for the way I was being treated. I was being treated less amicably than the dirt beneath his feet. He seemed to be deliberately provoking me into more and more rage.

I felt defenseless, but I screamed right back at him. Before long, it was a power struggle. I believed the devil was sitting there with a score sheet. I wasn't even sure of what "disproving Satan's veracity" meant, but I was sure that I was doing it again. My father's behavior was a sure indication of *that.*

On that particular night, my sister's dog, Cassie, was running around the living room in vicious circles, as usual, and it reminded me of what was happening in my mind. Al Peterson had no more respect for me than he would have for a dog. Therefore, I thought I *was* a dog, and I told my parents I was.

"You have put this family through hell, and I'm not going to let you destroy me!" My father kept yelling, as if I were doing it on purpose, as if I had plotted to deliberately destroy him. Many times he told me that I was the talk of the town.

My mother feared that I might do harm to my father, so she took me over to Community Hospital and made arrangements for me to spend the night so that they could get me committed to Mercy Hospital the next day.

CHAPTER FOURTEEN

MY CAREER AS A MENTAL PATIENT

My caseworker was different this time. Her name was Carol Preston. Dr. Garcia was my psychiatrist, and my psychologist was Bill Crouse.

I was not too obsessed with the unpardonable sin during this hospitalization, so I was transferred to an open ward within a week. I guess you could say that I had gone back to Harrisburg State Hospital for a visit. Within a month, I was discharged.

* * *

Not long before I left Mrs. Spring, I was driving my car out to my parents' home one afternoon, and spotted a man on a bicycle. It was John Wadsworth, one of Al Peterson's old friends. I stopped to talk to him. He asked me out.

Not long after the day I stopped to talk to John, we were going out every weekend. He went to the family reunion with me. He took me out on nice dates, and I thought I was in love with him. I got pregnant in October, and John was furious.

By November I was desperate.

I tried to give myself an abortion with a knitting needle. Three days later, John came to see me. I was having a spontaneous abortion. He took me to a nearby hospital, where I was admitted.

That same day, John came back after being gone for a while. I asked for some water, which the nurse was supposed to bring. John had a cupful in his hands. He kept telling me I looked thirsty.

"Have a drink," he kept saying.

I believe that he slipped me a Mickey, because within minutes after he left, I was so crazy I couldn't tell the difference between my hallucinations and reality. I was severely disoriented, and I thought I had blasphemed the Holy Spirit again.

John came to see me one time before I was transferred to Mercy Hospital.

"I know the reason behind all this confusion," I told him.

"What?"

"Satan."

"What is it, voodoo?"

"Satan is the author of confusion," I said.

At that, John left. I didn't see him again until a month or so later.

* * *

My sister believed that I hated her, and that was why I had such a grim attitude about her and her predicament. The truth of the matter was that I wanted so much more for her than to see her messed-up life like my own. I wanted her to recognize her responsibility in the matter.

Our parents were the ones who made us feel like premarital sex was an unpardonable sin, as was having a baby out of wedlock or getting pregnant before marriage. Now I know how sinful premarital sex is. The point is, our pregnancies were hidden from our parents because we thought we could predict their reactions. In reality, their reactions were surprising. They said that we didn't have to get married unless we wanted to, and that they would help us raise the children.

Mom was prepared to help me initiate a paternity suit against John, but I told her that I did not want anything from him, and that he'd never see the child.

Losing the baby was an act of God. I'm sure He felt I would be in no mental condition to care for an infant.

I think that my lack of compassion for Peggy's pregnancy

stemmed from my jealousy. She had a beautiful baby girl named Arielle Caroline, who looks just like her—and I lost *my* baby. I felt like less of a woman as a result. Although I had been in the same desperate situation my sister must have endured—not really wanting my baby. To this day, I feel saddened when a family member has a baby. I can't help but wonder whether my baby had been a boy or a girl. I think about names I would have given it. I wonder whether it would have looked like John or me. Would it have had brown eyes or green eyes?

Deep in my heart, I know that my baby had a soul, and even though he or she had no chance of survival, I know that my child's soul is with God.

This was just one of the many problems I discussed with my parents, my social worker, an Asian woman I'll call Ming, and privately with Chaplain Blackwell, or "Jess," as I called him. By this time we were on a first-name basis. I also discussed these problems with Lew (short for Luigi Cicarelli, my psychologist), who didn't feel they were relevant to my current crisis. Jess and the rest of the treatment team helped patch me up and send me out again.

CHAPTER FIFTEEN

MORE MANIPULATION

My first day at the CRR (Community Residential Rehabilitation) consisted of signing my life away.

After that, it was all routine. I was told that I had to go to partial hospitalization or find a volunteer job to structure my time during the day. Two other women and I took turns cooking and buying groceries. We also alternated cleaning the rooms of half the house. One side consisted of us females, and on the other side lived three men. I needed to structure my days because of all the idle time in the hospital.

I went to "Partial," an all-day therapy program, for about three months. That wasn't my cup of tea, so I got a volunteer job at the Salvation Army. My duties included sweeping and mopping floors, dusting, washing dishes, and sorting clothes. I used to do my share of malingering, which meant that I could lie in bed from morning until night. Even this didn't suit me, so about eight months after moving into CRR, I went back to the hospital. How did I accomplish the move? I overdosed.

I was manipulating the system.

I was admitted to Mercy Hospital, where I spent the next two weeks in the psychiatric unit. There my manipulative tactic was detected. Not only that, but my obsession-compulsion with the unpardonable sin resurfaced. Diane Mitchell, one of the psychiatric nurses, put it this way: "Gloria, you're working very hard to make yourself sick."

I *was* sick, but was I doing it intentionally? This made me angry—had Diane struck a nerve? Someone had once told me that a person would have to work very hard at blaspheming the Holy Spirit. Was that what I was doing? I used things that people said to build up a case against myself. I even asked people if I seemed to be evil. Yet, I was terrified of God. I so feared going to hell that when I heard God, the Holy Spirit, or Jesus Christ being spoken of reverently, I cringed in fear. Yet, when the Trinity was being spoken of *ir*reverently (which, by the way, is not often heard of the Holy Spirit), I was disturbed by it—a sure indication of the Holy Spirit's work in my heart.

I was, however, too busy worrying about the unpardonable sin to notice what was happening. I was the only person I knew who used the Holy Spirit's name in vain, although I never did it out loud. I believed God has protective spiritual laws that prevent a Christian from cursing the Holy Spirit, and in my case I had the aggravation of being mentally ill, and therefore unaccountable in God's eyes.

I was condemning myself. I really did want to get better, so I requested to be transferred to Harrisburg State Hospital. I said I wanted to go there because Chaplain Blackwell would help me. I worshiped him. It was a form of idolatry.

I was transferred to State Hospital the next day. The first thing Dr. Garcia said was, "Are you trying to drive me crazy? I send you home feeling okay, and you come back a few months later a mess. What are you doing? Playing a game?"

* * *

This time, Dr. Garcia actually allowed me to choose my own medication on the basis of my earlier experiences. Then he said, "Keep in mind that you're stuck with it once you pick it." I chose Taractan, a tranquilizer. I had taken it during a previous hospitalization, and it had made a big difference in my captivity by evil thoughts about God and the Holy Spirit. I thought it might produce the same results, but my head started feeling mushy.

I remember very little about this hospitalization—after the first six or seven admissions, it seems like one great big one. It was easier for me to say "I was in Harrisburg State Hospital for the best part of five years" than to try to recall thirty different hospitalizations. After a while, I lost count. I do know that I was in six hospitals over a seven-year period.

Ming was perhaps the most concerned social worker I'd ever had. She and Lew, along with Chaplain Blackwell and the rest of the treatment team, made great strides in helping not only me, but my parents as well.

Lew suggested that I might be suffering from an illness known as borderline personality disorder. He told me that people who suffer from this illness will manipulate their environment, do things to get attention, threaten suicide, and prove hard to satisfy. He said they are often looking for a perfect mother, perfect world, or perfect whatever. He said they have great difficulty with interpersonal relationships, and they're sometimes psychotic. This was a different slant to my problem that I had not heard before. Was it possible that Lew was right?

Dr. Garcia did not agree with Lew's diagnosis, but that did not mean that Lew was wrong. They simply had different opinions.

Approximately halfway through my hospitalization, Mom, Dad, and I started family therapy with Ming, my caseworker. Johnny and Peggy were asked to participate, but they said they couldn't because of "other obligations." I believe they declined because they were afraid they might discover some of their own weaknesses and have to take responsibility for their actions—something many adults never do.

My brother, I believe, doesn't even know what he is made of, let alone understand what motivated him to do the things he did. He was quite content to live in ignorance regarding my mental problems. He went to family therapy when I was seeing a therapist named Roy Trojan, and he was thoroughly convinced that Roy insinuated that he was "screwed up." My guess is that Roy either struck a few nerves with him, or he was in need of a convenient excuse not to participate in something that made him uncomfortable.

Johnny claimed that my illness hurt him too badly and that was why he quit coming over to the hospital with our parents to visit.

Mom and Dad had started coming once during the week instead of on Sundays, which was Johnny's day with our father. Not once did Johnny come to visit me on his own. I surmised that his annual Christmas Day visit to the State Hospital was by pure accident, but I will give him the benefit of the doubt. Maybe Mom or Dad coaxed him.

Peggy came to see me at the State Hospital *one* time. I later discovered that she had been coaxed. She was eight months pregnant and had gotten married all in the same month. Mom made Peggy come to see me because Mom wanted me to see her belly.

Peggy had problems of her own. She was still a senior in high school, and was eight months pregnant. Not only that, but she had conceived with a man who was not the man she married, and her husband knew it.

I was discharged just a few days before Peggy's baby was born. She wanted to quit school because she didn't want to face her classmates, friends, teachers, and so on.

One day I screamed at her, *"It wasn't as if you were raped!"*

Perhaps I hadn't handled my own pregnancy any more responsibly (with the knitting needle). Not only that, but I, too, was careless about birth control. I hated to cut Peggy down by comparison, but at least I kept a record of my periods, the dates on which they occurred, etc., and it didn't take four months to realize I was pregnant—I knew it instantly. I wondered if the girl could have been delirious for four months. And I did not get another guy to marry me who was not the father of my child.

Perhaps what angered me the most about my sister's predicament was that it reminded me of my own foolish lifestyle years before and a few months before.

I believe I was the one who told Peggy not to engage in sexual intercourse until she was old enough to accept the responsibility of birth control. Today, my advice would stem from a contrasting moral stance, but I think that this was good advice—considering that it was coming from a nonbeliever.

CHAPTER SIXTEEN

MY FIRST APARTMENT

In between group homes and mental hospitals—December 1, 1985, to be exact—I convinced my parents to accept the fact that I needed the opportunity to take a stab at independent living. I lied to my mother and told her that the staff at the group home said I was ready to move out.

Mom caught me in this prevarication, but still agreed to give me a chance to prove myself. I found an apartment in a small village only three miles from my parents' house. It was owned by Vic Brown, an uncle to Larry Brown, an old flame. The rent was cheap: all utilities were paid except electricity, which ran between $10 and $15 a month, and although it was nothing fancy, it was my first apartment, and I was very proud of it.

The first few weeks seemed like comfort and luxury to me—living alone, with no one to answer to, no curfew, etc. I didn't have to share the bathroom with anyone. I could eat what I wanted, when I wanted to, and if I wanted to let the dishes pile up for three days, I could get away with it. I had been under someone else's control—other than the Holy Spirit's—for so long I had forgotten what it was like to be free. The last time I was free was when my parents and my sister had gone to the shore for a week over the Fourth of July in 1980, and I had the whole house to myself for a week.

In spite of the freedom, I got very lonely, so I invited Kate Hill, a good friend of mine, to stay with me at my apartment one night. She slept on the couch and I slept in the bedroom. Just when I was falling asleep (about one o'clock in the morning), I screamed at the top of my lungs, *"Kate! Kate!"*

I believed that someone had shaken my bed.

Kate told me that right at the time I screamed, she looked up and saw what looked like the shadow of a man's body walking out of my bedroom. She said it was darker than the rest of the hallway. There were no men in the apartment, and all the venetian blinds were down. And the shades were pulled in my bedroom.

Morning after morning at exactly one o'clock, I was awakened by my shaking bed. Ray Lowmiller, the owner of the supermarket across the road, told me that a man had murdered his wife there. I was skeptical about ghosts until I moved into this spooked little dwelling, which had a coldness about it that I had never encountered before in my life.

Again, I talked to Ray about the apartment. He told me it had been a chicken coop at one time. He also told me that the murderer had killed a dog to silence.

I heard a dog under my bed. Eerily, it was at exactly one o'clock in the morning. I had no dogs, because pets were not allowed.

One morning at exactly one o'clock, I looked down across the foot of my bed and saw chicken feathers all over the floor. I had been sleeping with the hall light on, thinking that I was, in fact, having a hypnopompic hallucination, as the staff at Mercy Hospital had me convinced was happening. I thought that if I also turned my bedroom light on, I would see the chicken feathers.

I explained all of this to Dr. Pontious, my psychiatrist. He placed me on a potent tranquilizer called Mellaril to help me sleep and told me to cut all caffeine from my diet.

I bought two huge jugs of decaffeinated coffee, took the Mellaril as prescribed, and was in a semi-comatose state for three months. (I was actually "zonked out" most of the time.) I had to force myself to stay awake until exactly one o'clock so I wouldn't be awakened by my shaking bed.

I could not even get my mother to stay there with me.

One morning at exactly one o'clock, I felt like there was someone staring at me, so I woke up after having my bed shaken. I looked up and saw what appeared to be the apparition of a man, and although I could not actually hear the laughter, I knew that the ghost—the man—the demonic spirit—the figment of my imagination—was laughing at me. (I had heard half a dozen or so different explanations for what I was experiencing.)

I got up and turned on the light after lying there—petrified—for an hour.

Morning after morning at exactly 1:15 a.m., I'd call my mom and tell her to come get me because that damned ghost would shake my bed all night long. I tried moving to the couch, and the couch would shake. The television turned on by itself in the middle of the night on one occasion—at one o'clock, to be exact.

After six months in this miniature chamber of horrors, and I was admitted to Mercy Hospital on a voluntary basis. My speech was rapid. I also believed I was headed for hell because of the unpardonable sin.

CHAPTER SEVENTEEN

INSTITUTIONALIZED

The first thing I did when I arrived at Mercy Hospital was to seek out Christians to talk to. I went up to one girl, Donna, whom I knew from one of the Christian organizations in which I volunteered. I asked Donna if I had blasphemed the Holy Spirit.

"Ask *Him* to tell you," she replied.

For several days I thought about what she said, and finally I got good and mad at myself. I hated what I was doing to God, to myself, and to my family. I was only twenty-five years old, and all I had to show for it was a stack of psychiatric records as tall as I was (5' 11"), what I considered to be an impaired relationship with Jesus Christ, and feeling unloved and uncared for by my family.

I was bent on self-destruction. No human being could withstand the hell I had put myself through without experiencing lasting psychological, physical, and possibly spiritual damage. I had lost count of the number of times I tried to manipulate the system by hurting myself or taking overdoses. It's my belief that if I had truly wanted to die, I would have made a serious attempt to commit suicide.

At twenty-five,, I had a succession of scars on the inside of my left arm that resembled a railroad track. I carefully examined the mess I had made of my life, and thought more and more about what the girl from American Rescue Workers said. I knew I had to make a move toward the Lord, but I didn't know how.

One of the male aides at Mercy Hospital was going to try a behavioral-modification approach to my therapy, which he called

"FAKE IT UNTIL YOU MAKE IT."

Basically, he explained to me that I was institutionalized—that I was a walking, talking pharmacological encyclopedia and psychiatric textbook, and that I would be on a merit system in which I would receive rewards such as cigarettes.

The whole idea frightened me. I remembered what the girl said about asking God to tell me if I had committed the unpardonable sin, so I did it. The next day, I got good and mad at myself.

"Gloria!" I yelled as I walked up the hall. All of the nurses and aides wondered what was happening. I then went and lay down on my bed, face buried in my pillow, and cried out *"Your will, Lord, not mine!"* and meant ever word of it from the bottom of my heart. I'd said it a million times before, but this time I was truly sincere. I truly desired His will with all my heart. I saw the awesome depth of my sin, and was open to change.

Before all of this transpired, I had made arrangements to be transferred to the State Hospital in Harrisburg. I went there again to get my medication changed as my goal for treatment.

When I reached Harrisburg State, Rick Sascawiecz, my caseworker, asked me a question to which I gave a peculiar reply.

"Gloria, what is your value on a scale of 1 to 10?"

"Zero," I said.

"How do you rate at a zero on a scale of 1 to 10?"

"I feel like a worthless hunk of dirt."

He then told me that Vince, an ex-boyfriend whom my family despised, was there.

"How's he doing?" I perked up. I knew I had really hurt Vince, but I also knew that I could not go back to him.

I saw him at breakfast one or two days later. I went over and talked to him. He had a crew cut and was almost fifty pounds heavier than he was the last time I'd seen him, which was when I visited him at Gratesford State Penitentiary.

Vince had come to visit me two weeks before my birthday. He had bought himself a car, which he was so proud of.

He wanted to make love to me, which was probably the sole

intent of his visit.

I told him "No."

"You want to wait until you get married."

"Right," I said.

"I don't blame you," he said. At that, he left, but before he left, he told me that he would come to see me on my birthday, September 13.

I was at a spiritual peak with Jesus Christ at that particular time. It was my belief that the Lord had blessed me with the gift of divine healing and wisdom, and had made a "soul winner" out of me. My mission in life was to love and serve Him, no matter what the cost.

There was a young girl named Deidre Knight who had really grown to love me. She looked up to me because, as she put it, "You know a lot about life."

Deidre's boyfriend, Paul, was a soul hunter for a satanic cult. I hated the very sight of him. I vaguely remember being involved with him on a friendly level. I believed that his demonic power had blinded my mind, so I could not remember the involvement in its entirety. All I can remember are bits and pieces.

As I recall, I did not have sexual intercourse with Paul.

I was mentally ill and "in love with" the Lord at the same time. I shared the gospel with everyone who looked as though they needed a friend.

I believe Paul used me to create a diversion in an effort to keep Deidre from hearing the truth about Jesus Christ. He was a wicked man.

One day, one of the patients, Sally Kohler, was in dire need of a healing. She had a skin condition on her neck and arms. I called her into my room and rubbed my right hand over her arms. The Lord healed her instantly. Her neck was still dry and scaly, so I gave her Avon combination lotion and told her to rub it on her neck for three days, and then return it to me. She came back in three days with the bottle, and her neck had healed also. The poor thing was too sick to realize that she had been healed.

Demons attacked my mind daily while I was at Harrisburg State Hospital. Unfortunately, I was too young in the faith to know what to do about them. I later learned from Chaplain Blackwell that I could take authority over the demons in the name of Jesus.

There was an old man by the name of Manley whom I was always asking if I truly cared about my soul. In spite of my spiritual high, I still had my doubts at times concerning the unpardonable sin.

Manley's perpetual reply was, "I thought your soles was what was on the bottoms of your feet."

I hadn't tried to instruct him any further, but now I wish I had. Either the man wanted to know what a soul is, or he was ignorant of spiritual things. Any way you look at it, God's mercy extended to poor old Manley also.

There was a young man I had befriended on the hospital grounds by the name of Danny Riddell. We spent most of our time together during grounds-card hours. We talked about God, the meaning of life, the reasons for suffering, and so on.

Danny's hands were malformed, and he was bitter at God for making him that way. I tried to explain that his malformed hands were the result of an accident of nature, and that God was constantly offering him His courage to help him live with his disability. I walked into the recreation room one day and found Danny and one of his friends laughing. Naturally, I thought they were laughing at *me*. Danny said, "The wind is blowing."

"Why are you persecuting me?" I asked. I then ran out the door.

That evening on the grounds, Danny told me that whenever he was around me, he felt like he was carrying something heavy on his back, and that his knees were going to give out on him.

I thought it had something to do with the Lord's either making Danny carry his cross, or perhaps he was going through the same thing Saul of Tarsus experienced, so I told him the story:

"Saul of Tarsus was a Pharisee who put Christians to death, persecuted the church, and was trying to overthrow the kingdom of God.

"One day on the road to Damascus, he fell flat on his face and the Lord said

to him, 'Saul, why are you persecuting me'?

"Saul asked, 'Who are you, Lord'?

" 'I am Jesus, whom you are persecuting.' "

All of a sudden, Danny fell down and said he had to turn the cross around.

I believe the Lord speaking through me got Danny to realize that we serve a risen Savior.

He used to tell me that he had the love of God in his heart.

Danny had an obsession with thinking he was blaspheming the Holy Spirit. He also wanted to die. He tried to commit suicide on several occasions. Like me, he had a history of drug and alcohol abuse.

The only difference between Danny and me was that Danny thought he saw Christ in an acid trip.

I wanted to be healed of my schizophrenic disorder, so three times I asked God to heal me. Three days later, I saw Christ at the very moment a verse from the Bible went through my mind—"My grace is sufficient for thee."[4] I *knew* it was Him.

One day during this hospitalization, Danny and I shared a bench on the hospital grounds.

I said to him, "I think it is God's will for us to escape from this hospital."

"Don't you think we should pray about it? Where would we go?"

I said the Lord's Prayer.

"I don't think we should do it," Danny said. "We could get in a lot of trouble."

"Well then, I'll go by myself."

"Gloria," he said, "I care about you. I don't think you should do it."

Minutes later, I left the hospital grounds. I walked up a road that

---

4   From 2 Corinthians 12:9, (KJV)

ran parallel to the hospital and encountered a man, who asked me if I needed a ride. His name was Cam Pifer.

"Do you know where the Narrows is?" I asked.

"Sure. I'll take you there."

I had my Bible with me, and I said, "I want to spread the gospel all over the world."

"Did you come from the State Hospital?"

"Yes. Why?"

"I'd better take you back, then."

He took me back to the hospital, and I was sent back to the closed ward. I read in my Bible about how Judas betrayed Christ. I thought I was Judas and that *I* had betrayed Christ.

From the hospital, I moved into another CRR home. This living arrangement lasted a month or so, just long enough for me to get a volunteer job at American Rescue Workers, have my gall bladder removed, and return to my parents' house, where my mother could satisfy her maternal instincts and nurse me back to health.

I went back to Mercy Hospital approximately two weeks later, because once again I thought I had blasphemed the Holy Spirit.

CHAPTER EIGHTEEN

THE DEVIL'S STRONGHOLD

After returning to the ward, I lost my grounds-card and within the next couple of days signed myself out against medical advice.

One day I was uttering those blasphemous words under my breath. This bothered me. Why couldn't I stop? I told God that I wished I had never known anything about the unpardonable sin, that I wished that I was totally ignorant of it. Then I said, "I commit it to You."

I picked up the Bible and started reading. The print seemed darker on some words than on others. Again, I was convinced that by saying "I commit it to You," I had committed the unpardonable sin. I then found myself doing things that would have suggested that I was *trying* to commit the unpardonable sin.

I called my father on the phone and told him what I had done.

"When are you going to quit playing games with God?" he said, in a very angry tone.

I hung up the phone, went to my room, and started reading my Bible again. Again some words were darker than others.

Was the Lord trying to tell me something?

Since I was supposed to be discharged three days after signing the discharge paper, I had to find a place to go. So I called Ron Day, a Christian attorney I knew from my hometown. Ron made arrangements for me to go to a posh hotel for five days, with the Salvation Army providing the money. He said he would come to pick me up either that night or the next day.

In the meantime, I called my own room at the hotel to see if I was there. I literally felt like I was somewhere else. There was a noise that sounded like water dripping on a microphone, only I thought it was Vince's sperm. He had said something about getting a room at the Spencer Dauphin, a nice nearby hotel. Was he playing a game with me? I was really paranoid.

I somehow became convinced that I had invented the atom smasher, and I told everyone.

One of the nurses piped up and said, "The atom smasher has already been invented."

I believed I was "behind the cross" of Jesus, only I did not feel safe. I truly believed I would someday commit the unpardonable sin, if I hadn't already. I believed I was headed straight for hell, so I tore up my discharge papers.

That Saturday at approximately 11:00 a.m., I was told that I had visitors. A few minutes later, in walked Ron Day and Josey Van Horn, an old friend of mine.

We sat down, and I wasn't making sense at all.

"I need the Spencer Dauphin," I said. "Vince jacked off in a microphone. His brother was in on it. I invented the atom smasher. I hope I never lay eyes on him again as long as I live. I hate his guts."

"Gloria," said Ron, "you told me no one here cared about you. The lady who let us in seems to care about you a lot."

Ron and Josey seemed relieved that I had destroyed my discharge papers. I was absolutely mentally disturbed. If I had left the hospital, I probably would have been dead within days.

* * *

At around ten o'clock Tuesday morning, Dr. Garcia called me into the nurses' station. By this time I was experiencing the worst sort of depression I'd ever felt in my life. I told him I was spiritually dead.

Dr. Garcia changed my medication to Loxitane and Lithium. I had been walking around delusional for almost three months, and he wasn't even aware of it. (People who are truly psychotic are not usually aware of it. Besides that, the doctor was reportedly an alcoholic who came to work only when he felt like it. He's back in his homeland of Peru now, having been deported.) In fact, I had talked to him only one other time during the entire hospitalization.

I was seeing "demons" all over the carpet, the pages of my Bible, etc., so one day I tore my Bible into several pieces and threw them into the trash can.

One of the patients was shocked to see me doing this, but I said, "It's got demons all over it that tell me I blasphemed the Holy Spirit and that I'm an evil-minded wretch."

She looked at me as if to say, "I understand."

* * *

Feeling hopeless and so depressed that I just wanted to die, I went to my room, found a mirror in my makeup bag, broke it in half, and slashed my left wrist. I did not require any stitches until a few days later, when I took a pencil, stuck it in the biggest lesion on my wrist, and ripped it so hard that the pencil lead broke off underneath the skin.

Dr. Garcia instituted a court hearing after that.

My attorney, Mr. Shore, talked to me a few minutes before the hearing. We decided that he should not seek permission for me to go through the behavior-modification program at Mercy Hospital after my court-ordered commitment was over, when forty-five days would have passed.

In the meantime, the demons continued to pop up out of the carpet. There were demons plastered all over the pages of the Gideon Bible I was using, and I was convinced that God was punishing me for committing the unpardonable sin.

One night I drank a bottle of shampoo, and, as a result, was locked up in seclusion. It just made me sick as a dog and gave me diarrhea.

I wanted to die, and I was determined to kill myself. I didn't care how I had to do it. In fact, on one occasion, I tried to hang myself with my shoestrings.

I was desperate to die, but I couldn't find a way to do it.

* * *

Forty-five days passed. I was scheduled to go to Mercy Hospital, but I didn't feel like going anymore. I just wanted to commit suicide and get it over with. Dr. Garcia said I had to go; that was the way the court petition was worded. So off we went—the driver from the State Hospital, one of the psychiatric aides, and me—to Mercy Hospital.

When we got there, we sat in the waiting room for almost an hour, after which Dr. Pontious came down to talk to us. The psychiatric nurse handed him my file. He leafed through it and said that I was in no condition to leave the State Hospital.

The aide explained that the court petition stated that I was to spend the second half of my commitment at Mercy. Dr. Pontious had no other choice but to admit me.

I went upstairs and within hours tried to slice my wrist with a toothpaste tube. Two days later I was back at Harrisburg State. Dr. Pontious and Dr. A., an Indian doctor who was treating me, said they had no other choice because the unit was overcrowded and understaffed. Besides, I was a danger to myself.

When I got back to Harrisburg, the Christmas tree was up, as were all the decorations, but somehow I didn't even care about Christmas that year. That's because in addition to those decorations, the tables, the floors, the windows were all decorated with demons. I cried out for the Lord to help me, just as I had been doing for days.

Suddenly I looked around—everywhere there had been demons, the face of Christ now appeared between the demons and me.

Christ held a cross up.

I assumed that the cross meant there was refuge for me in the cross of Jesus.

The Lord loved me. He was reassuring me of His love for me, and that His help was still available to me. This gave me comfort, and I realized that I had not committed the unpardonable sin for a while.

Christmas came.

My parents brought my presents, as they always did. My brother came also. I was still very sick, but I knew I had not committed the unpardonable sin.

I was happier than I had been for years on that Christmas morning, but as soon as Mom and Dad and my brother left, I began to be stressed again, and again I felt the compulsion to say those words about the Holy Spirit under my breath. Again, I felt hopeless. I rushed into my room and drank a bottle of hair conditioner. After I got it all down, I went and told the nurse what I had done.

"You *didn't!*" she said.

I was taken to a nearby hospital in the State Hospital ambulance. There they made me drink a gallon of water. We went back to the State Hospital, where I was again locked up in seclusion. Again, I got diarrhea and was sick to my stomach. I was out of seclusion in four hours.

The following Tuesday, Dr. Garcia came on the ward. When he reached my name, this time around he asked to speak to me. He was utterly disgusted with me "for playing these games."

I went through forty-five more days of psychotherapy, journal writing, life skills, and group-therapy sessions with my psychologist, Bill Crouse, and other aspects of my therapy.

At the end of forty-five days, I was discharged to a CRR called a Supermax, a group home for low-functioning adults with mental problems.

I recognized many of the clients there from the State Hospital and other hospitals I had been in. One was Gordon Smythe, whom everyone teased. Gordon was always pounding his head; he was pathetic. Another was Mike Pysher, an obese young man with red hair who did things for attention—calling in bomb scares, trying to commit suicide, etc. He had been in mental hospitals and jails half a dozen times by the time he was nineteen. There was a guy named Ray Moore, whose father was a federal judge. Ray told me that John Wadsworth had also ruined his life with drugs. The sad part of it is that Ray lasted in the group home for only a few weeks; because of his explosive temper, his father put him in a private mental institution in Florida. I believed what Ray told me because John admitted it to me himself.

Other female residents of the group home included Phyllis Harrison, Pastor Yeager's sister-in-law. Phyllis was in Harrisburg State Hospital the same time I was. Then there was Sarah Eiswerth, who was also from State Hospital. (She lasted only a few weeks.) Finally I recognized a girl by the name of Mary Guthrie, who had been in Danville.

Our regimen consisted of taking turns cooking, doing the cleaning once a week, and day programming, which took place over in the male wing. This Supermax was different from the other group homes in this area. A woman named Barb Fenster coordinated a variety of different groups and activities, and she brought a video camera several times. She recorded Mary Guthrie and me doing a skit on good manners. There were cooking groups, group therapy, and games in addition to going to movies and bowling.

We had to be over in the male wing by 8:00 in the morning, and the house had to be immaculate. Thursdays were grocery days. We took turns doing this also.

I lasted in this setting a whole two weeks, after which time my obsession-compulsion with the unpardonable sin resurfaced, and I was taken to a hospital about fifty miles away. This one had a very small psychiatric unit, half the size of Mercy's. I had a psychiatrist, Dr. Russell, who squinted a lot and couldn't sit still. I thought he had more problems than I did.

Here is what Dr. Russell wrote concerning my mental status while I was a patient there:

"Patient is cooperative to the interview. In the examination, she frequently interrupted the exam by saying that she wanted to see the hospital chaplain. She is of the Protestant faith. She looks at me with some exaggerated eye contact. It is hard to tell if she is looking at me or looking over my shoulder. She sits rather straight and had very little body movement when she talks. There was some inflection in her voice, but it is less than normal. It has a somewhat monotone quality. She answers questions asked. She will add little bits of information, but not much. Her clothing and hygiene appear appropriate."

In addition to my mental status, Dr. Russell wrote a note regarding my content of thought:

"The patient states that she has visual hallucinations all the time, and these are of demons talking to her, and they look like little faces that often smile and float around, and they comment on her behavior. She has heard the devil and demons talking to her, and they are critical of her behavior but they only talked to her once in the last six months. She denies that the voices give her directions, and she denies following any directions that the voices or what she sees may give her. She states that she frequently hears people talking to her from the TV and radio. She denies that they give her any direction."

As for my insight:

"The patient has intellectual understanding as to why she is here. She has little emotional insight, why she did the things in the past would lead her to many hospitalizations and eventually here."

Dr. Russell stated in his notes that I could answer questions of similarity and problem-solving well. As for proverbs, he stated that I could do rather well on some, not too well on others, and that some proverbs I would just not try to interpret at all.

My diagnosis was chronic paranoid schizophrenia. A diagnosis that one, believe it or not, that I had heard only once before. To me, in any case, diagnoses were important. I had always been a collector of opinions. There was one opinion that suffered, however—my opinion of *myself.* My parents felt very much alone in what they were going through with me. My mother, in particular, felt all of the emotional anguish that *I* felt, if not more. Dad felt that even the church had abandoned him. No one seemed to know how to comfort them. But I wasn't helping matters, either. As a manipulator, I was making myself much sicker than I really was.

My brother and sister like to say that I did not try hard enough. I wonder how they would have reacted had the circumstances been reversed? Would they have even survived?

I was a patient at Memorial Hospital only five days before I was transferred to Harrisburg State Hospital again.

CHAPTER NINETEEN

MY FINAL HOSPITALIZATION AT HARRISBURG STATE

When I went to Harrisburg State Hospital on March 25, 1987, for the last time, Dr. Garcia was again frustrated. He may have even felt angry. He was always saying, "I let you out of here. You say you feel fine, and a few weeks later you come back a mess." In a way, I felt sorry for him, but thus far, neither he nor the hospital staff had gotten to the root of the problem.

Within a week of being admitted, I had a grounds-card and wasted no time going to Chaplain Blackwell's office. The first thing I said to him was "I left this place on March 2 and took my compulsion with me."

Chaplain Blackwell said, "I had a feeling that was what happened."

A few days later I went up to his office again, and he said, "Glo, I hated to see you suffer any longer with your obsession and other aspects of your illness, so I asked God to heal you. For the next few weeks, or as long as it takes, whatever you see, hear, or think, if it makes you feel better, if it builds you up in the faith, and if it adds to your wholeness, it's for you. Anything that upsets you, or makes you feel worse, is not for you."

A special surge of love was placed in my heart by the Holy Spirit. Chaplain Blackwell kept saying, "Let your heart teach your head." I wasn't quite sure what he meant by this then, but I soon found out. The love in my heart was there to straighten out the thoughts in my mind.

In the next few weeks, the Lord gave me thoughts that were

to build me up in the faith, make me feel better, and add to my wholeness.

One night, I had this thought—only it sounded like a voice: *Think happy thoughts.* It was definitely of the Lord. I went home on a weekend pass, and something my brother said struck me as coming from the Lord. He was recalling some things that had happened to us when we were children—*good* times. Then he said, "That's the kind of things you want to think about." I looked at a picture of one of my nieces on the television, and in the picture, she appeared to be saying, "I love you, Aunt Gloria."

The following Monday morning, after I had returned from my weekend pass, I reported to Chaplain Blackwell. I told him what the Lord had said, and what my brother had said, and about the picture of my niece.

"Praise God!" he said. "Thank you, Jesus!"

Later that day, I was talking to a young Mennonite girl who had been a patient at State Hospital longer than I had. Anna was a very sick young woman, but she had also participated in the Lord's healing of my obsession and psychosis.

I told her I had felt I had committed the unpardonable sin for so long that it had become second nature to me.

She said, "You can't keep worrying about that any longer. You have to let your heart teach your mind."

I reported to Chaplain Blackwell immediately after I finished talking to Anna and   told him what she had said.

"Thank you, Anna," he said. "You're open to the will of God, and you didn't even know it.

"Praise the Lord!" he said again.

Chaplain Blackwell went on vacation for a few weeks. Chaplain Corson was instructed to talk to me at least once a week. He was made aware of my situation—that the will of God was for my healing and that He was using Christians and personnel all over the hospital to accomplish this task. Chaplain Corson was one of the assistant chaplains who were working there only part-time, so our visits were limited.

One day in his office, I noticed a huge picture of Jesus Christ holding a little girl. I marveled at it. "Where did you get this picture?" I asked. It reminded me of the time before I had received Christ as my Savior when the Lord said, "Come unto me as a little child."

"Do you like that?" he asked, and I nodded. "Who do you think that little girl is?"

"Me."

"What do you think Jesus is saying to you?"

"He's saying 'I love you.' " I had even seen his lips moving in the picture as He said it.

"And He will *always* love you," said Chaplain Corson.

The Bible played a big role in my return to a lifestyle free of the obsession with the unpardonable sin during my last hospitalization at State Hospital. The Lord gave me verses that added to my wholeness, made me feel better, and built me up in the faith. Anything that was contrary to "the formula" was not for me.

I would be obsessed with the unpardonable sin, pick up my Bible, and begin to read.

I will never leave thee, nor forsake thee[5] or *Lo, I am with you always, even unto the end of the world..*[6]

Sometimes the Lord would speak to my heart through the Word, as if to say, *I will never, never leave thee nor forsake thee.* If I felt tempted, the Lord gave me this verse: "Blessed is the one who perseveres under trial because, having stood the test, that person will receive the crown of life that God has promised to those who love Him."[7] Psalm 121 was also a frequent means of comfort and assurance the Lord used. And there were many others.

Chaplain Blackwell and I had to get to the root of my problems.

It was suggested that I was terrified of my earthly father, whom I also loved; therefore I was also terrified of my heavenly Father,

---

5   From Hebrews 13:5 (KJV).
6   From Matthew 28:20 (KJV).
7   From James 1:12 (NIV).

of whom man was made an image. In other words, the fear I had associated with the unpardonable sin sprang from a distorted perception of what God is like. Although my earthly father was not physically abusive to me, he was verbally abusive—especially during my periods of insanity.

I perceived God as being ready to pounce on me the minute I did something wrong.

Because of Chaplain Blackwell's persevering attitude toward my recovery, I came to realize that both of the other members of the Trinity are like Jesus. The chaplain urged me to read the Gospels to find out what Jesus is really like. As a result of finding out what He is really like, I came to realize that the Holy Spirit's character is just like that of Jesus Christ's. He is understanding, loving, faithful, patient, kind, humble, peace-loving and gentle, and He is a healer. He is everything that Christ is.

The Holy Spirit committed Himself to be with me always, just as the Lord did. What applied to one member of the Trinity applies to the others.

CHAPTER TWENTY

A NORMAL LIFE

I went back to the CRR from Harrisburg State Hospital on May 26, 1987, only this time, the group homes were run by a different company. Some procedures had changed—for example, staff members now took us to the grocery store instead of having to drag a grocery cart up the street. My long-distance telephone calls were restricted to two per week. And I had an intolerable roommate named Judy C.

One night, I forgot one of the items on the grocery list, and the girl was a raving maniac over it. Another time I got Dole raisins instead of Sun-Maid, a fate worse than death.

Judy was a 5'2" bully, but she soon met her 5'11" match. I gave her a dose of her own medicine. By the end of two months, we were bullying each other so badly practically every minute of the day that I requested to be moved to a different home. Granted, I might have found someone worse than Judy, but at this point I didn't believe anyone *could* be worse than Judy. Judy was the pits.

They had a vacancy right up the street, and I moved within days. Before I left, I yelled through the door at Judy, "I don't know of anyone else who could stand to live in the same house with you, either!"

My new roommates, Marian B. and Fran D., proved to be very nice people, with a few exceptions. Marian smoked from four to five packs of cigarettes a day—a ridiculous habit even for a heavy smoker. Fran, on the other hand, was a grossly obese person who had a distinctive odor, particularly true of her for a certain week of the month. At those times, one had to use the bathroom without breathing. Fortunately, Fran moved out within a few months.

This particular group home did feel like home for the most part. I went to my parents' home on weekends just to break the monotony. I had a problem with the telephone, which made it necessary for the resident program supervisor to get the long distance on the phone disconnected on the female side. They said they did it for my own good, to save me some money.

On February 25, 1988, I was admitted to the psychiatric unit at Mercy Hospital. As with many of my hospitalizations, I wanted to get away from my surroundings. I merely manipulated my environment to get what I wanted.

This time I had a female doctor, whom I will call Dr. C.

Dr. C. was a sharp cookie. None of the other patients who were assigned to her liked her, but I did. I thought she looked like Barbara Feldon, who played Agent 99 on *Get Smart*, and seemed to know me like a book after talking to me for only fifteen minutes.

Dr. C. diagnosed me as having a borderline personality disorder and a schizophrenic disorder. Here are some of the notes she wrote:

"Youngish twenty-seven-year-old with obviously subdued and flattened affects in spite of a presentation suggesting an underlying vivacious personality . . . religious preoccupations . . . suicidal ideation . . . speech otherwise logical and coherent. No hallucinations or delusions . . . overvalued ideas . . . no homicidal tendencies. She describes visual images of a frightening 'devilish' face and of lights upon closing her eyes—these fade in time and are not clinically classic visual hallucinations.

"Impression: Schizophrenic Disorder' Borderline Personality Disorder and good capacity for insight. She can benefit from psychotherapy.—She has the capacity—when recovering from this acute decompensation."

Bill Hatcher, my social worker, wrote as follows on February 29, 1988:

"Gloria was admitted to the IPU on 2/25/88 on a voluntary basis, has an extensive psychiatric history since the age of 15 with multiple admissions to this facility and to Harrisburg State Hospital. Gloria was last treated at this facility from 9/15/87 to 10/1/87 under the care of Dr. A. Greenawalt with a diagnosis of Schizoaffective Schizophrenia with Bipolar Psychotic Features."

The admission was relatively short. I returned to the group home and went on with the daily routine, only to land in a Pittsburgh hospital a few months later.

I was going to a rehabilitation school where I behaved like a morally decent human being for about three days. On the third day I met Guillermo Torres. Everyone called him "G.T.," and this was the beginning of a nightmare.

To me, G.T. was someone I needed at the time to feel like I belonged. I was in a strange place, after all, where I hardly knew anyone. I was in bed with G.T. the first day I met him. I was behaving just as I had when I was "of the world."

I told G.T. that I no longer drank or smoked dope, and on the second day we were together, I did it anyway. Up to this point, I really believed that I had conquered my drug and alcohol problem. As a result of the marijuana, I experienced a highly bizarre reaction—I believed everyone around me had a Spanish accent.

On the third day that G.T. and I were together, we went to luxurious downtown Pittsburgh, supposedly to buy some sun block, cigarettes, and other things. We did buy these things, but when we were finished, G.T. wanted to go to the liquor store. It was there that he bought a liter of vodka. We drank a large part of it on the city bus back to school, having mixed it with Pepsi. We finished it off in the woods near the school. I can vaguely remember taking half my clothes off.

G.T. yelled, "You better straighten out!"

"Get the hell out of here!" I screamed.

Then he said, "You're crazy!"

I said, "Guillermo *el asno,* maybe you've met your match. (*Asno* is Spanish for *ass.*) Now get out of here!"

I struggled to put my clothes back on but didn't do a very good job. One of my socks was missing. My blouse was unbuttoned, and I was covered with mud. I hated myself so badly for the things that had happened in the three days I had spent with G.T. that I banged my head on a rock until I had a black-and-blue mark.

I started toward the road and passed out along the side of it before I got to the rehab school. One of the officials called an ambulance. The nurse from the school asked me what had happened, and I told her I had been raped. When we arrived at the hospital, they asked me if I had been raped, and I denied it.

They put me on IVs, and while I was lying on the litter I kept staring at the security guard. I told him I didn't like his looks, then went toward him and tried to punch him in the face. Within seconds I found myself in four-point restraints, where I remained for the next 24 hours. The psychiatrist, Dr. Franklin, was not the most amiable psychiatrist I'd ever met. One day after I was allowed out of the restraints, he threatened to put me back in them just for giving him a piece of my mind. I discovered that Dr. Franklin was the type of doctor who didn't take any guff. He felt that I had made a foolish mistake by drinking all of that alcohol. In fact, it could have cost me my life.

I told him that all human beings are deserving of respect.

"Especially when they start showing some respect for *themselves,*" he said.

I had to admit that he had a point.

I was a patient in this hospital for five days. Dr. Franklin was going to court-commit me to Harrisburg State, but I explained to him that if he would only send me directly to the group home, I would go to Alcoholics Anonymous often and continue in partial hospitalization. He agreed to my idea, and I was home in a matter of hours.

I got back in touch with G.T., and we made plans to live together. But over the phone and in correspondence the relationship failed, which to me was a blessing in disguise. G.T. didn't want me to look at other men, talk to other men, etc. As for the alcohol and the marijuana, he said he gave it to me to test me, to see if it was easy for me to lie. In reality G.T. was a Class A idiot as well as another "charming creep," as Dr. Pontious would say.

Life went on in the group home, and on August 1,1988, I moved out. I ran an ad in the paper to reside with an "elderly Christian couple," a situation where I would do housework in exchange for room and board. Out of a dozen or so responses, I was impressed with only two or three. One of them was a widower who had lost his wife a year before. Another was just what I was looking for, except for one minor detail. The couple had not attended church in over seventeen years because they felt the church was after their money. I could sense they were very greedy, since they wanted $200 a month to live with them and do housework, too. Finally, there was an old man living in a trailer in the country whom I later moved in with.

This living arrangement lasted exactly one week. He told me not to haul people in his car, which I did. He expected more work out of me than I performed. He caught me going over the speed limit once, which made him furious. It was almost the straw that broke the camel's back. The engine also burned up one night on my way back from a former boyfriend's house, and it made the old codger so angry that I knew if I stayed I'd be in for a perpetual picnic.

One night I had a coughing fit that caused one of my ribs to crack. I had no driving privileges the next day, so I called an ambulance to take me to the hospital. The crack in my rib failed to show up on the x-ray, but Dr. French, the emergency room doctor, said I seemed very depressed. He wanted to take me to a social worker who was with the psychiatric department in that hospital.

The social worker talked to me briefly and got me a voucher for a cab that would take me to the Carroll Building, where I was to see Mary Johnson-Bush, my caseworker. When I arrived, she told me she wouldn't be able to see me for two and a half hours. By then I was angry, frustrated, and utterly upset all at the same time. I really believed that she knew I was coming and that she would be ready to talk to me. With the things that had happened with the old man and now this, I was going to get some help one way or another, so I went in the bathroom and swallowed all the medication, which consisted of ten to twelve Loxitane capsules, thirty or more Lithium pills, and forty-five pills or so of Thorazine. It may have appeared to be a manipulative gesture on my part—and in fact this was so—but at the same time I was stressed out. I *did* take the overdose to get Mary's attention, but I was also angry, frustrated, and upset at the same time.

No one else seemed to be helping matters either.

I was placed in the care of Dr. D., who transferred me to the psychiatric unit at Memorial Hospital. I remained there for about five days under the care of Dr. Landon.

Dr. Landon thought I might be primarily manic-depressive. He said this because he thought I was getting better rather than worse, which he said is generally what happens with schizophrenics.

Here is what Dr. Landon wrote in his discharge summary:

"Gloria is a large woman who has lots of intellectual insight about how she uses overdosing to get attention, about how she cannot tolerate delay, but actually is an easy and chatty person at this point. She does not seem psychotic, nor is she suffering from hallucinations or obvious delusional thinking at the time of admission. She knows that she will have to get out of the hospital rapidly and hopes to get into a more stable living situation."

I was discharged on August 8, 1988, after I made arrangements to rent an apartment from a dear Christian lady who had been my friend for almost ten years.

CHAPTER TWENTY-ONE

WORKING AT WHOLENESS

I moved into my apartment on August 10, 1988, with my dear Christian friend Marianne Jackson as my landlady. Marianne would turn out to be much more than a friend—more like a mother who loves and loves and never judges or condemns. She treats me to lunch on occasion even now, and she remembers me on my birthday and holidays. She has listened to my problems when no one else would, and she has always found time to talk.

On September 1, 1988, I signed a contract with Mary Johnson-Bush, my caseworker—my own idea. The purpose of the contract was to keep me from manipulating the system, keep me busy, and limit my calls to Crisis Intervention. It lasted about six months, after which it was no longer necessary because I had started living up to these goals independently.

I had started keeping a journal on August 27 of that year. Although I didn't write in it steadily, I did so in spurts. I also copied in it some outstanding letters that I had written to a variety of people. In one of them I documented a relationship I had had with a guy who was also a mental patient. Here are some excerpts from my journal:

January 13, 1989
I've had a man in my life since before Christmas. His name is Robert Carl Scott, Jr. Actually, we've been friends for a long time (11 years), but we only recently got romantically involved.
. . . This damned "Reaganomics" doesn't give us people on dis-

*ability enough to even own a car, and if you are fortunate enough
to be able to own one, you can't have a nice one because you
can't have more than $1,500 or so in assets. I can't get out of this
poverty rut. The only jobs it's possible to get pay minimum wage,
and I need at least $7.00 an hour to pay for medicine, rent, phone,
electric, and so I can own a car. I have no incentive to work at all.*

*. . . I hate life. When Mom and Dad are gone, I'll have to go to
an institution or something. As far as my brother and sister are
concerned, I do not even exist. I worry about what will happen
to me when Mom and Dad are gone all the time. I will succumb.
I will commit suicide. I need someone to share my life with, but
it will probably never be "Spike" (Robert Scott). He has already
made that clear to me.*

* * *

It's true that Johnny and Peggy have never been very supportive
of me. In fact, my sister insinuated by her actions and the things
she says that she is clearly ashamed of me. If I could have a dollar for each time she came to visit me at my apartment, I'd have
enough money for three packs of cigarettes and a candy bar. If I
had a dollar for each time my *brother* came to see me, I'd have
enough money for *two* packs of cigarettes and a candy bar. (I forget to mention that I am referring to Pyramid Lights, which cost
$.75 a pack.)

My sister and I were never close, but I have made an effort to
reach out to her in recent years. She really doesn't want my love.
I have also made an effort to reach out to my brother, but he has
been non-receptive as well. You cannot force yourself on people;
they're either going to desire your friendship or not.

When I lived in a city that was only fourteen miles away, my
sister and brother claimed it was too far to travel. Now I live only
five miles away from them, and they still don't come around. My
brother remarked one time, "Well, it's been so long"—referring to
when I first got sick.

"I've been doing well for over a year," I said. "Now, what's your excuse?"

As for my sister, I wrote her several letters expressing my views. She never so much as acknowledged receiving them.

I called her to discuss one of my letters with her.

"Why can't you treat me this way all the time?" she said.

I think she secretly wanted me to prove myself to her. Who did she think she is—*God?*

I didn't have to answer to her. I had but one authority, Jesus Christ, our Lord. He was the one who was healing me. I sincerely doubted that my sister even prayed for me; it probably never occurred to her. This was just an educated guess, not necessarily the truth.

She was always in such a hurry, and the only time she went to see our parents was when she didn't want to cook or needed a babysitter.

Who was I to expect more from her than she gave her very own mother?

Life wasn't the same as it used to be. I remember going to visit uncles, aunts, and cousins for Sunday dinner. Now these same uncles, aunts, and cousins ignored me on the street—they would look right at me and tell me they didn't see me. They never did this before I was diagnosed as a schizophrenic.

My maternal grandmother was so cruel to me that I often felt that she must have *hated* me. I reminded her of my mother's father, also a schizophrenic, and in a mental hospital for practically half his life. (I think what she was doing is called "transference of aggression.") She verbally abused me every time I went to her house.

I lost some friends as a result of my illness, and I gained some. I learned that true friends will stick by you, no matter what.

As for relationships with men, I had no desire to get married at that point.

I wanted to make that decision when I was 100 percent well.

Here are some examples of what certain relationships were like:

January 22, 1989

Although Spike and I are semi-together, I don't feel the same way about him as I used to. I cannot go on with this charade. It has to be a clean break unless Spike shapes up. I love Spike, but there's no future in it, so I'd better end it.

Spike and I were together for a little over a month. He was so incredibly despicable and obnoxious. He delighted in his insanity. He never took any medication, but it was never his fault when they carted him off to the VA Hospital. It was always because he was poisoned or just a victim of the system.

The guy literally believes his own lies.

By now, the reader is probably wondering what I saw in Spike. The truth of the matter is that I was lonely, and he was there.

For six months in early 1989, I had a volunteer job at Meals on Wheels, which made me feel wanted and needed. I took a leave of absence to work on this book and to babysit a neighbor's child for a few months. It proved to be an unfruitful arrangement in more ways than one. I have not been much of a "people person" in recent years.

CHAPTER TWENTY-TWO

TWENTY-PLUS YEARS AND HOLDING

Since I was required to structure my days while I was living in a group home, I chose to volunteer at a soup kitchen. I do not volunteer anymore. I have arthritis so bad that I cannot sit or stand for long periods of time.

This is where I met J.J., the man who would become my husband.

Over a four-year period, we encountered each other frequently. Finally, he asked me to go out with him. After our second or third date, I knew I would never be able to get rid of him. Not only that, I had no *desire* to get rid of him.

J.J. was so very different from the men of my past. He treated me with dignity and respect. He would never deliberately set out to hurt me or anyone else.

A few months into our relationship, we went out to dinner at Kentucky Fried Chicken. It was there—believe it or not!—that J.J. got down on one knee and asked me to marry him. I told him to call me in three days and I would give him my answer.

"Do you mean to tell me," he replied, "I got dirt all over my pant leg just so you could put me off for three days?"

Three days came around, and J.J. and I got married on September 12, 1991.

No one in my family believed I would make it down the aisle. In fact, I had always said that if I weren't married by the time I was 32, I would never get married at all. But guess what? It really wasn't planned that way, but we got married the day before my

32nd birthday!

During the first year of our marriage, we gave each other anniversary cards on the 12th of each month.

Since we never had any children, J.J. and I have compensated for that by spoiling our nieces and nephew. Christmas has always been special. We've been told not to spend all of our money on the children, but we do it anyway.

We couldn't be together one Christmas because I was in the State Hospital. Everyone except the children—Mom, Dad, J.J., Johnny, my sister-in-law, and my sister—brought Christmas to me.

J.J. and I did experience some marital problems. At one point, my mental health issues were starting to wear him down, and his parole officer even suggested that he get an annulment. During a disastrous home visit one weekend, J.J. had to have me court-committed because my symptoms were surfacing. But somehow the two of us worked through our problems together.

My mother had heard about an experimental drug, Clozaril, that doctors were having good results with in treating schizophrenia. She insisted that Dr. Garcia try it as an alternative medication.

There was one problem, though. I had to go through withdrawal from all the other medications I had been taking. For a period of time, I was completely psychotic. Then, the psychiatrist began administering Clozaril.

Shortly after starting Clozaril, I began drooling on my pillow at night. Eventually I found a way of controlling this complication. I tried sleeping on my back instead of on my side, and it worked.

I have been on this drug for seventeen years now. I firmly believe that God and medicine work together.

Not only that, but I believe that a familial support system—mostly my husband— makes life more tolerable than having to live alone.

With God's faithfulness and that of my husband J.J., I expect never to be alone.

* * *

Over the past twenty years, J.J. and I have been best friends. He loves my family, and we all love him.

J.J. must have excellent coping skills, since I am not the easiest person in the world to get along with at times. I've had to do a certain amount of growing up in the past ten years or more—I've learned that I can't change the people in my life. *I* am the one who has had to do the changing.

Both J.J. and I are recovering alcoholics. We have been a support system for each other.

Our relationship works. We have no desire to hurt each other. As for myself, my love for J.J. is coupled with a sense of gratitude. He has given me so much—not necessarily material things, either. In emotional terms, it's give-and-take, day by day.

Volunteer work is something I have positive feelings about. At Manorcare Nursing Home I taught elderly ladies how to knit. I also helped prepare food for cooking at St. Anthony's Center. Obviously it paid nothing, but it made me feel like I was pulling my own weight.

I enjoy knitting, which helps me earn a few bucks here and there. I am especially busy at Christmastime. It's become a tradition for me to knit dishcloths for the women in the church congregation. I've made several afghans for friends and family, and scarves and hats and slippers. I've made two sweaters for J.J.

Jigsaw puzzles help me to kill time, especially during the hibernation of winter months. I have glued some of them together already, and they are hanging in my living room.

J.J. and I enjoy entertaining guests. Most of our friends are members of the church that we attend. My culinary specialty is lasagna, but I also make a mean spaghetti and meatballs.

J.J. and I like walking in the evenings, especially through Brandon Park. Hurr's Dairy is close by. It's not unusual for us to get an ice cream cone, sit under a tree, and watch the squirrels.

Our twenty-first anniversary will be coming up in just a few months. We've been together for over two decades. Some of the time it's been very hard, but most of the time it's been happy in important ways. Every day is a challenge, yes, but we meet it as best we can.

Would it have been possible without medical assistance? Certainly not.

Would it have been possible without J.J. at my side and the support of my long-suffering parents, who've had major health problems of their own to deal with? I don't think so.

Would it have been possible without the guidance and inspiration of my Savior, Jesus Christ?

No way.

No way but His way.

www.ingramcontent.com/pod-product-compliance
Lightning Source LLC
Chambersburg PA
CBHW031327040426
42443CB00005B/241